Chico and the Coach

Chico and the Coach

Herman J. Valdes

XULON PRESS

Xulon Press
2301 Lucien Way #415
Maitland, FL 32751
407.339.4217
www.xulonpress.com

Dictated By: Herman J. Valdes
Edited By: Elizabeth Abbott, Emily Stoops and Betty Valdes
Book Cover and Illustrations Designed By: Austin Janowsky
Technical Assistance: Allison Humenansky

Printed in the United States of America.

ISBN-13: 978-1-6628-1246-0
Hardcover: 978-1-6628-1247-7
Ebook: 978-1-6628-1248-4

Book Inspiration

MY PURPOSE IN WRITING THIS book was to fulfill a life-long dream of capturing a life that was lost and through my acceptance of Christ and my father's guidance, was changed; thus influencing my life and my teaching and coaching career. I wanted to share with others specific incidents and life experiences that they might not make the same mistakes. Through my story I hope others would be inspired to live up to their true potential in Christ.

TABLE OF CONTENTS

Who Was Chico?

HI! I'M HERMAN VALDES. AMONG other titles, I'm also called "Dad", "Granddad", or "Grandpa." To many in the community, I'm "Coach Valdes" or just plain "Coach." My story begins with a glimpse into the life of my father, Eusebio Valdes. Throughout his life, he was known as "Chico" and then as "Chico the Barber." Later, he became "Chico the Preacher."

Chico was born in Ybor City (Palmetto area) to Spanish-speaking parents, who came to America from Cuba in the early 1900s. They were cigar makers in Ybor City and alternated between residing and working in Ybor City and Cuba. For a time, they spent six months of the year in each place. Chico spent most of his boyhood years in Cuba and was cutting hair there at the age of 13. When he was about 15 or 16, his father, Nicolas, died, and the family moved back to

Tampa permanently. At that time, Chico became employed as a barber by the Minardi family. They owned a barbershop on Grand Central Avenue in Tampa.

Chico met my mother, Esperanza, at a dance held at Ballast Point Park in Tampa. Weekly dances were held for young people. They were married in 1935 and moved to New York around 1936 or 1937 to seek better employment opportunities. While in New York, Dad served in the Merchant Marines for a period of time. After I was born in 1940 and unwilling to cope any longer with the weather in New York, they moved back to Florida. They lived in Key West the first time. Dad was a barber at the La Concha Hotel. There was a naval base in Key West, and he kept busy by cutting the hair of many sailors.

The family then relocated to Tampa. This is where they made their home. Chico, my dad, got a job working in St. Petersburg for what was then the world's largest drugstore, Webb's City. At the barbershop, there were 20 some barbers. Dad was one of the most recently hired out of those 20. At that time, haircuts were 35 cents. He was able to keep 20 cents of that. In order to survive, he had to cut many heads of hair each day.

After working long hours, Dad would drive all the way back to West Tampa where we lived. The drive across the Gandy Bridge was dark and lonely. Chico thought a lot about life during those drives. He was a tough guy. He loved to drink, even though I never saw him drunk. I learned that he carried a barber razor in his sock for protection. This was before he accepted Christ. He was a good father, a good husband, and a good provider. Though we were never what one would consider wealthy by any means, we never lacked for anything. In fact, my father was very generous and provided not only for his immediate family but for relatives who transitioned from New York to Tampa and needed a place to stay. He somehow managed to make it all work.

During the time Chico worked at Webb's City, a man came in and sat in his barber chair. Chico put a cape around the man's neck and prepared to cut his hair.

The man asked, "Chico, if you died today, would you go to heaven?"

Chico responded, "What the hell business is it of yours?"

Dad proceeded to cut the man's hair, removed the cape, and sent the man on his way. Months later, this same man returned.

He said to Dad, "Have you thought about what I asked you several months ago?"

That was the beginning of a relationship that led Chico to accept Jesus Christ as his Lord and Savior.

During his unsaved days, Dad liked his liquor. Alcohol was a temporary relief from his restlessness. He began searching for an inner peace, and he thought, perhaps, religion might hold the answer. In 1955, he was still the same drinking, cursing, and gambling barber that he had always been. There was only one place left for him to look–the Bible. Several passages in the New Testament caught his attention. He read those over and over. In between, he had met a Methodist minister. This minister challenged him with salvation and was the individual who had confronted him with salvation while at Webb's City.

In response to an advertisement he had seen, Chico and Mom decided to attend an evangelistic service being held at the Tampa Gospel Auditorium. Both ended up responding to an invitation to receive Christ. Dad was 41 at the time. After his conversion, there was a radical change in his life.

Shortly after his conversion, Dad began attending Tampa Heights United Methodist Church. Soon, he was teaching a Spanish Sunday school class there. He and Mom did this together. This class grew and grew. Eventually, the leadership of the Church came to him to inform him that he could no longer teach that class because he did not have the proper credentials. So, I like to say that the Methodists gave him the right foot of fellowship, and he was on his way out. A Baptist church then took an interest in Chico.

He was a tireless worker. His life began to change in many ways. He began visiting hospitals, teaching Sunday school, preaching, and counseling Cuban refugees. He did all this while working full time as a barber.

Since Dad no longer drank with the other barbers he worked with in St. Petersburg, they felt he had deserted them. He cleaned up his language and was a constant rebuke to the cussing of the other barbers. Chico no longer participated in gambling with cards on paydays, as was the custom at the barbershop. He began to feel ostracized by the other barbers. They were undermining his customer's confidence, causing him to lose clientele. He felt it was time for a change.

Caption: Chico with daughter, Hope and wife, Esperanza.

Chico had a home, a wife, and two children to provide for. He was encouraged to seek the Lord for help. Certainly, God could meet his needs. Time went on. One evening, he received a call from a woman he did not know. She had heard of his conversion and asked if he would like to open his own barbershop. She offered to lend him $1,500, interest-free, to help him get started. This was a new beginning for him. He believed it was an answered prayer. He was now able to open his own barbershop on Bay to Bay Avenue in South Tampa.

Chico studying the Bible at his Bay to Bay barbershop.

When forced to close the shop on Bay to Bay because of construction of the Expressway, Dad opened a barbershop in the Bayside Building east of MacDill Avenue off Bay to Bay. He worked from 8 a.m. to 5 p.m. each day. He would spend hours studying God's word in a program called the Academy of the Air. After completing this course and receiving his diploma, the pastor of Hope Christian and Missionary Alliance Church in Tampa contacted him and asked if he would start a weekly Bible study class in Spanish. The class flourished and attendance grew and grew.

Chico then sought additional training through the correspondence school of Emmaus Bible School in Oak Park, Illinois. He received a diploma from Emmaus, and he became involved with the Emmanuel Baptist Church of Tampa. He was ordained on July 29, 1959. All the while, he continued to teach the Spanish Bible class at the Alliance Church.

Chico had only a formal third-grade education. However, he was a bright man and a hard worker; actually, he was a workaholic. He would cut scripture from his Bible and paste it in his notes in order to prepare lessons and sermons. He was doing "cut and paste" before computers were even in use. He typed using only one finger. His sermons were always challenging and exciting. Dad took some additional biblical studies courses at Toccoa Bible Institute. Eventually, he and Mom started a church of their own, the First Spanish Baptist Church. They pastored for over 30 years. From time to time, Chico also preached in front of many large congregations. He had an accent, and I think people listened more closely as a result.

Let me share with you some of Dad's unusual driving habits. His idea of a Sunday drive was to take off from home and drive for miles and miles with no particular destination in mind. It was not uncommon on a Sunday after dinner to drive to Black Point to catch a ferry that would take us across Tampa Bay to Bradenton, as the Skyway Bridge had not yet been built. Then, we would come home by US 41. We would just make a big circle.

On one occasion, I remember that a member of the family in New York passed away. Mom wanted to be there to support the family, so they packed several suitcases and off we drove to New York. There were no interstates at the time. We drove up Highway 301 and just drove and drove and drove. Chico didn't know what it was to take a break, to stop and rest, or to stop overnight to break up the trip. He had a Thermos full of some heavy-duty black coffee to keep him alert, and I was the coffee boy. As a young man, I remember crying for Dad to stop, so we could rest, sleep, or maybe get something to eat.

He would only say, "Shut your mouth. Give me some coffee."

It was nothing for Dad to drive literally 10, 12, or even what seemed like 15 hours without a break, stopping for gas only. I recall one particular Sunday drive, traveling from Tampa to Key West. My mom and her mother, Anna, were born there. Dad had worked there at one time as well. There was sort of a connection that drew us down to Key West on occasion.

At the time, the only major road to Key West was US 41 through the Seminole Indian Villages. There were no rest stops, gas stations, or places to eat between Naples and Homestead. If you got to Homestead after 5 or 6 p.m., all the gas stations would have already closed, forcing you to spend the night if you were low on fuel. On more than one occasion, we got caught in that situation. I remember Mom putting cheesecloth in the windows of the car to keep the insects out. Mom was not very happy with that situation. I was not either. On some of these trips, my sister, Hope, was there. I know she wasn't happy either. The next morning, we would drive to Key West, look at the old homestead, maybe have lunch, turn around, and drive back home. This was definitely insane.

Before Dad became a pastor, he was led by the Holy Spirit and at the invitation of Orlando Corwin, a missionary in Colombia, to go on a mission trip to the Andes Mountains in South America to minister to some of the Indians living there. He went to a bank in Ybor City and proceeded to fill out the paperwork for a loan to finance the trip. The loan officer wanted to know what he would use for collateral. Dad, at that point, asked to speak to one of the bank officers. He told the bank officer that God sent him there, and the money was going to be used for a mission trip.

The bank wrote him a check. He left his family and caught a plane to Miami. The next stop was Barranquilla, South America, and from there by mule back to the top of the Andes Mountains. At the time, we didn't know exactly where he was, how to reach him, when he was coming back, or if he was even coming back. I was a college student, and I was not saved. I could not understand why he would do such a thing. I tell people today that if the Baker Act had been in effect during that time, I would have used it on him.

During this trip to Colombia, Dad told the story of how he led an Indian woman to Christ. She wanted to express her thanks in the best way she knew, so she gave him a large section of handwoven rope. Confused, he stared at it, wondering why she had given it to him. She explained that she had made the rope 11 years ago for her son's hammock. The son left, and she had not seen him since. She wanted Dad to have it. Moved by her gift, Dad never let her know that he did not sleep in a hammock. Instead, he thanked the woman for the gift and offered to pray for her son's return.

On his return to Tampa from that missionary trip, many local churches invited Dad to speak and share his slides and other interesting artifacts he brought back. Free will offerings were collected to help cover his expenses. Instead of using the money for himself, he used it for another missionary he had met in South America. This missionary had been walking on his mission trips for 20 years. So, Dad sent the money to be applied towards the purchase of a Jeep.

In the summer of 1962, Chico felt God would again have him minister in Colombia, South America, with the missionary, Orlando Corwin. This time, it would be for a period of three weeks. Chico conducted evangelistic services in rugged mountain country. He traveled by Jeep, journeying deep into the Andes Mountains over territory that became so rough that it could only be traveled by mule back.

On this second mission, Chico met the same woman who had given him the hand-braided rope and whose missing son he had promised to pray for. She greeted Chico with the good news that her son had returned, and she was overjoyed. It was now her prayer that her son would accept Jesus Christ as his Lord and Savior.

On this same trip, Chico also encountered the missionary he had sent money to for the purchase of a Jeep. The missionary, however, felt that the natives needed a church building worse than he needed a Jeep. He claimed he had been walking for 20 years and could continue to do so. Chico was taken to the village where the new church building was established. He was amazed at the commitment of some missionaries, as each devoted their entire lives to ministering to the Indians.

While on this trip, Chico was scheduled to be one of the main speakers at a four-day conference held in Fonseca, Colombia. He became ill after the conference, but he pushed on to travel thousands of feet up the Sierra Nevada de Santo Marta Mountains to minister to the Kogi Indians. His guide served as his interpreter on this trip up the mountains. Dad related that he had led one particular native to Christ, who vowed he would live with only one wife and would give up chewing the narcotic coca leaf. Many others also came to Christ on that trip. Chico fellowshipped and studied with these Indians and with others he had led to Christ the previous year.

Caption: Chico ministering to Indians in South America.

On returning to Barranquilla from the mountains, Chico was not feeling well and was exhausted. Coming down the mountain on a mule, he let the mule carry him at its own pace. His guide was ahead of him. It had rained, and the narrow trail was slippery and had a drop-off of 3,000 feet straight down. The mule he was riding, usually as surefooted as a mountain goat, suddenly slipped. Two of its feet dropped over the edge of the cliff. As soon as he felt the mule go down, Chico instinctively gave it a jerk, and its feet immediately came back up onto the trail. Chico claimed it was nothing short of a miracle and immediately praised the Lord for his safety. When they reached a clearing, Chico's guide said he had glanced back, saw the animal go down, and then come right back up. It happened in mere seconds, yet it was an encounter with death that Dad never ceased to thank the Lord for His protection.

On his return to Tampa, Dad could not just sit back and relax. On Mondays, he visited the tuberculosis hospital. He witnessed and gave out tracts to the patients. On Tuesday evenings, the family attended prayer meetings at the church. On Wednesdays, Chico visited other hospitals, and Mom would frequently accompany him. He still devoted Thursday evenings to the Alliance Bible class.

Later, Dad took on responsibilities among the Spanish-speaking people of Armenia Baptist Church. There, he preached and conducted a service every Sunday morning and evening and a midweek prayer meeting. In between all of these ministries, Chico still managed to cut hair every week.

At the age of 51 and 10 years after being saved, Chico had led more than 500 people to Christ through his testimony and personal witnessing. As a barber and a preacher, much of Dad's ministry took place in the barbershop. One could never go into the barbershop without hearing the gospel of Jesus Christ being shared. Customers did not seem to mind that politics and baseball were not the main topics discussed in the shop.

I recall one incident Dad shared. One of his long-time customers came in for a haircut. This man was sad and depressed. Dad asked what the problem was. The man proceeded to tell Chico that he had just come from the funeral home where his brother had been cremated. He shared that there had been no preaching, no devotional of any kind, and no message or funeral service for his brother. He felt bad that none of those things had taken place.

The man had the urn with the ashes in his car.

Chico, being Chico, said, "Well, bring the ashes into the shop. We'll have a service for him right here."

That's exactly what they did. Anyone waiting for a haircut that day had to wait for the service to conclude.

Dad also performed a wedding in the barbershop. Steve, a young man Dad had known for a long time as a customer and who worked for an engineering firm located in the same building as the barbershop, brought his bride-to-be, Sandra, in and asked if Dad would marry the two. Dad agreed to do so. He performed the wedding right there. It turned out fine with about eight or nine people present. It even made the newspaper at the time.

As stated earlier, much of Dad's ministry took place in the barbershop. He has had people kneel at the foot of the barber chair and ask to be saved right there in the shop. Many came to him for counseling while getting their hair trimmed. If a person came in with a problem and wanted to discuss it privately, Dad would just lock the door and talk with the individual.

The barbershop was also Dad's office. He kept his Bible and many other religious books next to his typewriter in the barbershop. In between haircuts, he would type his sermons, all of which were delivered in Spanish. However, Sunday school classes for the children at his church were taught in English.

My dad was generous to a fault. Through my coaching and my relationship with athletes, he met the mother of two of my basketball players. This family lived in the projects, and the mom was the sole breadwinner, raising three physically large children. On occasion, my mom and dad would take groceries and other provisions as needed to assist them. This family loved my mom and dad. Eventually, dad practically gave away his car to this woman. She was so proud of that automobile and was extremely grateful to now have transportation.

One unusual happening in my dad's life was as follows. Dad had been ministering to an individual who was terminally ill, spending many hours sharing the gospel at the man's bedside. Before he died, the man instructed his family that upon his death they were to buy Chico any car that Chico wanted–any car.

To fully know the type of man that Chico was, you must know this. When the family came to share with Chico what the will stated, Dad chose a four-cylinder Mercury Zephyr.

I said, "Dad, why not a Cadillac or a Mercedes-Benz?"

Dad's response was, "This is all I need."

Chico, a man who led thousands to Christ and a barber with only a third-grade formal education, was the man in 1 Corinthians 1:27.

> "But God chose the foolish things of the world to shame the wise; God chose the weak things of the world to shame the strong...so that no one may boast before him." (1 Corinthians 1:27-29 NIV)

God always chooses the least likely. In many cases, it appears that way. There are many stories in the Bible that bear this out. Gideon, whose clan was the weakest in Manasseh, was the least in his family. There was Moses. He told God he was slow of speech. David was even considered one of the least. He was the youngest among his brothers and a small shepherd boy. He defeated Goliath and later became King. God always manages to choose the least likely, so no man can boast of himself but of the Lord.

Dad spent his last years before retiring as a barber at MacDill Air Force Base. He made many friends. Dad was a character. Often, people could not pronounce his given name, Eusebio. To help people remember him by the name of Chico, he would give them a saying they could remember.

"I'm Flattop Chico from Puerto Rico."

While some people live as if each day was their last day on Earth, Dad's life philosophy was that one should live each day as if it were the first day of the rest of their life. That is what he did until the very end, winning souls for Christ at every opportunity.

Chico died on the Palm Sunday of 1993 at the age of 79. I am including these next paragraphs and quoting word for word from some notes that Mom recorded on the day of my dad's passing. This is truly a love story.

Today, April 4, 1993, Daddy went to be with the Lord his Savior. Right up to the end, he talked with me. He told me how much he had loved me over the 58 years we had been married. He said I had been a very good wife and mother to his children. We kissed each other. He pointed his finger to the sky, and then he was gone. Daddy wanted to die at home, surrounded by his family. Daddy looked so beautiful and peaceful.

Rev. Bruce Williams spoke at a service held at the funeral home. Then, Daddy was taken to Herman's church, Bayshore United Methodist, and his wonderful son preached a wonderful message. Only with God's strength would he have been able to do this. The coffin was wrapped in an American flag. Everything was done just like Daddy wanted.

He was to be buried in the Veterans' Cemetery in Bushnell. He had a military service at the cemetery which I shall never forget so long as I live. Everything was so peaceful. I cry as I am writing this, but I know I will be seeing him again someday.

Daddy, we love you, and again I say that everything was done as you wanted. Your entire family and most of all, our two children, Herman and Hope, and I love you so much.

Mama

Growing Up in West Tampa

NOW, IT IS TIME FOR my story. I was born in New York City (Manhattan) on February 8, 1940, during one of the most severe snowstorms in the history of New York. Dad would often tell me that it got so cold in the apartment that he removed some of the cabinet doors to burn in the wood stove out of desperation and the need for warmth for a newborn baby. Mom and Dad moved to New York for job opportunities, even though Dad spoke little to no English at that time. All he could ask for in English was coffee, a slice of apple pie, and a glass of Coca-Cola. They ended up being so miserable that they contemplated moving to Key West, Florida, where my mother and grandmother were born. In case you're not aware, it's fairly warm in Key West. Having to burn cabinet doors is not at all a necessity. There was also a naval base there, and that interested my father. He became a barber at La Concha Hotel.

Dad loved to dance and act. Before he married my mother, he was dancing and acting on small stages in wintertime productions. It was a classic example of my father's crazy and wild side. This was opposite to my mother's very conservative nature. She was a stay-at-home mom due to her being an epileptic. Her fear of having a seizure in public was overwhelming. She never caught a bus to go to the mall or was willing to call for a taxi. She always depended on Dad to take her wherever she needed to go. Like most in the Latin community at that time, Dad was a barber and the sole breadwinner and provider for the family. I always felt this was the key to them getting along so well. They completed each other and relied on one another.

My mother once told me a story of my very first day of kindergarten in Key West. She walked me to school and returned home. Several hours later, I navigated myself back home.

Mom asked, "What are you doing here?"

I responded, "I've already learned it all."

Mom immediately walked me back to the school. She was amused at my explanation for leaving school. She was not that upset with me; however, she was alarmed that I had been able to leave school without the teacher having any knowledge that I was gone.

Herman at 4 years of age while living in Key West.

We moved to Tampa fromwwKey West. I remember living in an upstairs apartment with a balcony on Seventh Avenue in Ybor City. I recall going with Dad to get ration tickets for gas, food, and other provisions, as World War II was still going on. It was not long after that the war ended, and there was a great celebration up and down Seventh Avenue.

We later moved to West Tampa to 2714 Green Street. This was just a few blocks away from the Boys Club. During that time, our house had no air conditioning, no central heating, and unfortunately no hot running water. To heat the house, we had to use a kerosene heater, so our time in New York wasn't as far behind us as we had first thought. The kerosene heaters were not operated overnight for fear of fire, as our home was built with pine lumber imported from Cuba. In the wintertime, Mom would put newspapers between my blankets to insulate them; however, the newspaper made all kinds of noises as I tossed and turned in my bed.

Mom would have to heat water, making sure it was the right temperature for her boy to take a bath. She was very meticulous in that way, and that translated into our appearance as well. It was important to her that my shirts, Dad's shirts, and even our underwear were always ironed. As soon as the weather turned warm, I would walk to school, and Mom made sure that I had a fresh clean shirt. Of course, it was always ironed. We didn't wear tennis shoes or jeans. At the time, it was a sign of poverty to wear tennis shoes or blue jeans to school. Today, we spend more money on blue jeans and tennis shoes than we do on many of our dress clothes. It just shows you how times have changed.

When I was nine, my sister, Hope, was born. She was named after my mother. Mom had lost a child early in her marriage, so she was delighted to now have a baby girl. Hope became the "queen of the house."

As a child, I felt it was kind of strange to be named Herman John Valdes. I remember asking Mom about this when I was in middle school.

"Mom, wouldn't it have sounded better if my name was John Herman Valdes?"

She responded, "We had not yet chosen a name for you when you were born. The doctor attending the delivery was a tall, handsome, blonde-headed man. So, I asked the doctor what his name was. He told us it was Herman."

Mom decided right then and there. That's how I got named Herman.

I took a lot of abuse from my classmates because of the name Herman. There was a sausage company in Tampa named Herman's Wieners. You can see where all the boys kind of chimed in on this abuse. I'll never forget my ninth grade English teacher, Mrs. Knopf.

She said to me, "Herman, come here."

I walked towards her desk and responded, "Yes, ma'am."

She asked me if I knew what my name meant.

I said, "No ma'am."

She said, "Your name is Herman, pronounced *Errman*. It means leader, warrior, a leader of men."

My little chest just puffed out. From that point on, I had a feeling of confidence that I could be anything I chose to be. I still felt I had to fight every time the abuse began again, and I often got paddled for it.

I remember an incident in one high school class. The science teacher, Ms. Cason, was teaching a lesson on natural gas. She was attempting to demonstrate that it was odorless and tasteless. About that time, one of our classmates sprinkled some sulfur on the flames that heated the water in the radiator. When heated, sulfur gives off an awful odor, as if someone had passed gas (farted). The class broke out in laughter. It was quite difficult for the teacher to regroup. In fact, she also began to laugh with us. We were always up to some mischief. We were pranksters in high school. If you saw *Grease*, you can have an idea of how high school was during those times.

On the first day of my teaching assignment at Buchannan Junior High School, Ms. Cason ironically was one of the first faculty members to whom I was introduced.

She took one look at me and said, "OH NO! NOT YOU, AGAIN!"

When we lived on Green Street in West Tampa, I had a close friend, Eddie. We became buddies. We constantly competed in sports and got into mischief daily. I had a German

Shepherd and some rabbits. We had citrus trees, avocado trees, and mango trees that simulated a small grove.

Across the street at Eddie's house, they had a cow. During the day, Eddie's dad kept the cow in an empty lot that was two blocks away from the house. One day, Eddie and I, without telling anyone, decided to bring the cow from the lot to the stall where it slept. When Eddie's father went to get his cow, it was not there. He came home screaming in Spanish at Eddie and me.

"Mi vaca, mi vaca, donde esta mi vaca?" ("My cow, my cow, where is my cow?")

Little did he know, the cow was already in its stall! Needless to say, Eddie and I both got in trouble that day.

Boyhood friend Eddie, and Herman–partners in "cow caper."

The people of the neighborhood were so close. If you did something wrong, it would always get back to your mom and dad. Every person on the block had permission from your parents to correct you and to discipline you if necessary. It was a tight-knit community.

During this period, one of the best things that happened to my family was that the interstate needed to be built on our property and the property of all the people between the two streets at the front of our home. The government came in with the "right of eminent domain" and offered us a price for the house. The amount was not acceptable, so my father negotiated for a better price. On selling, we had to leave our beloved community, and our lives profoundly changed after that.

Shortly after selling the house on Green Street, Dad purchased a concrete block home on the corner of Chestnut and MacDill Avenue. This was a much nicer home, and my mom and my sister were happier there. It was such a blessing for my parents to live in that house.

I attended Jefferson High School from 1955 to 1958. I played basketball and football. Sports kept me quite busy. On the football field, we were very, very tough, but we were not very skilled. As I reflect, my experiences with coaches at the high school level were not incredibly positive. This would later affect me. When I began my coaching career, I was coaching the same way that I had been coached. I was physically aggressive and somewhat verbally abusive.

My tenth-grade year was my first year of high school. At that time, junior high school only included the seventh, eighth and ninth grades. Junior high was a scaled down version of the high school. In high school, I was a running back. To be specific, I was a fullback in the T-formation. I weighed 130 pounds when I started high school. By the time I graduated, I weighed 180 lbs.

Back then, you played one position. You didn't specialize. Today, we have a punting team, a receiving team, and a kickoff team. You have a punter and a field-goal kicker. Now, young men and women specialize in sports.

As a running back, I backed up a Division 1 prospect, Sam Rodriguez. Sam was big, strong, and powerful. He was recruited heavily at the next level. I was not getting much playing time. However, I had a very strong leg and ended up in the placekicker position. I kicked extra points and field goals, and I kicked off. I did get occasional playing time on special teams.

I remember that my mom and dad had not attended any of the games. In fact, they never even gave me official permission to play. I remember forging all the necessary documents. One day, they decided to come watch me play. Would you believe that at that game I got kicked in the arm and fractured a bone attempting to block a punt? From that point on, my only duties were to kick extra points. After I kicked the winning extra point against Chamberlain High School in a pre-Thanksgiving game, the student body nicknamed me the "Golden Toe."

Boys Club Adventures

A S I LOOK BACK ON my early years, it was the Boys Club that kept me out of trouble. It helped me develop into the person I am today, though I made many mistakes along the way. Boys Clubs are typically built-in areas of high delinquency. A Boys Club was built in West Tampa on the corner of MacDill Avenue and Laurel Street.

I spent a great deal of time at the Boys Club. I also volunteered to work there. My duties were to distribute athletic supporters (jock straps) and shorts to members who wanted to participate in activities in the gymnasium. For that, my compensation was free membership, a Royal Crown soda, and a moon pie. After some time, I was promoted to Gymnasium Assistant. With that title, I was involved in all of the sports programs and any other activities that were held in the gym.

Caption: *West Tampa Boys Club Basketball Team, early 1950's.*
Herman #10.

At this point in my life, many of my friends were becoming involved with drugs. This led them to commit theft and vandalism. I attribute that to a lack of structure and discipline in the family and poor use of their free time. My schedule was to go straight to work at the Boys Club right after school. Mom and Dad would bring my meals and make certain I would do my homework on the job. I made sure to stay busy. As I began to play sports in junior high and high school, I had practice first after school. Then, I would get to the Boys Club at about 6 p.m. and stay until 9 p.m. Mom and Dad would continue to bring my meals.

From the very beginning, I was introduced to two individuals at the Boys Club that helped mold my life: Charles "Stretch" Murphy and his wife, Ruth. Stretch had played basketball at Purdue and was an All-American team member in both basketball and volleyball. This was fitting for his 6' 9" stature which made him tower over the boys that were at the Club. One of his teammates in school was John Wooden, the legendary coach of UCLA.

Ruth Murphy introduced us to archery. Can you believe it? Her ability to get a bunch of boys, many of whom were delinquents, to learn the art of archery was a feat in and of itself. Yes, they turned us loose with bows and arrows. It was such a different time back then. Of course, the arrows found themselves flying in places where they should not have been, yet the learning continued. We were also introduced to rifle instructions. We used Red Ryder BB guns for target practice. That is how we got good enough to hit our targets from an assigned distance.

Herman (far right) Boy Scout Troop 38

I was a member of Boy Scout Troop 38. I gained the rank of Star. We would camp on the property of the Boys Club and would attend the yearly Boy Scout Jamborees at Bok Tower in Winter Haven, Florida. One year, we built a tower at the jamboree that must have been nearly three stories tall. It was amazing.

Just like with any troop, we sometimes got into mischief on campouts. One time, someone brought a BB gun. Throughout the evening, we took turns pelting some of the other Boy Scouts. On another occasion, there was a Boy Scout who was a heavy sleeper. He would sleep so deeply that no matter what we did we could not wake him. One night, we got six boys and put one at each corner of the tent, one in the front, and one in the back. On a given signal, we lifted the tent and relocated it. This left him out in the cold. It was so funny to see him squirm and turn and eventually look up to recognize that he had no roof over his head. We thought it was funny. He did not.

At one point, the Boys Club received the first trampoline donation in the city of Tampa. We had an instructor come in and teach us rebound tumbling skills. Boys being boys, we moved the trampoline near a basket and proceeded to hone our skills in the art of dunking the basketball. During one of those extremely excruciating dunks, my momentum carried me forward, and I flew off the trampoline. I ended up landing on the tile floor, causing my knees to swell immediately. It was severely painful, and I believe it is one of the reasons I have had to have two knee surgeries as an adult.

I met my wife of 60 years at the Boys Club, and I still consider it a strange happening to this day. When I first saw her, she was playing a Hawaiian steel guitar and singing Christmas carols for a music studio group. The studio performed at the annual Christmas party for the Boys Club. I was the curtain boy and was in charge of pulling the curtain across the stage that night. All the boys gave me a hard time by providing an over-exaggerated applause every time I walked across the stage. However, this beauty with a steel guitar caught my eye.

My wife Betty, Charlie Collins, and Marti Singleton in 1955, performing at Boys Club Christmas party where I first met Betty.

We began to call each other every night and go to the movies whenever we had some pocket change. On Saturday nights, we would go to the North Boulevard Recreation Center and dance. I seemed to take after my dad in that respect. Oh, how we loved to dance the night away!

Betty went to Madison Junior High School and lived in Port Tampa. It was fitting, as her dad was a tugboat captain at the time. Her mother was of Spanish descent. Her grandmother was an immigrant from Spain, and she loved me dearly.

At that time, I had no transportation other than my bicycle. Often, I would ride my bike over 12 miles to visit Betty. She went to Plant High School, and I went to Jefferson High School. We both graduated in 1958.

Betty turned down an academic scholarship to Florida State University. She was always a wonderful student and a scholar. She's a well-read woman even to this day. I, on the other hand, did not care much for school. In fact, I skipped more than my share of days from school. My dad used to tell me that one day God would punish me for skipping so much school and put me in school for the rest of my life. Little did I know, that would be true.

After graduating high school, I immediately went to work on the Howard Frankland Bridge in Tampa. My duties began on a pile driving barge, making $1.10 an hour and working 10 hours a day. I worked a few months on the bridge and began to determine that this was not my career for the rest of my life. I was injured on the job and ended up losing the tip to one of my fingers. After that, I asked myself an important question. Can a man do this kind of work when he's 60? I answered my own question after falling off the bridge three times. The answer was no.

Not Your Typical **College Years**

Oranges

Fish

I ASKED MYSELF ANOTHER IMPORTANT QUESTION. What do I need to do? Obviously, I needed to continue my education. How was I going to pay for it? The University of South Florida was not yet completed, so I could not attend there. There was an opening on the University of Tampa's basketball team. I decided to test my luck and try out for the team. I had turned down a basketball scholarship to Saint Leo College in Dade City because I was in love and did not want to leave my sweetheart. It was the same reason Betty turned down her academic scholarship to Florida State. So, we both started college together at the University of Tampa.

For my basketball tryout, I walked out onto the court and gave it my best shot. There was a young man, who had to be about 6' 8", trying out with me. He grabbed my rebound, swung his elbows, and hit me square in the jaw. I ended up bruising the inside of my mouth and loosening up a few teeth. I managed to keep them. There went that idea.

I still needed to fund my education. I was living at home and got a job working for the American Can Company. They made cans for all kinds of things–baby food, paint, orange juice, etc. They also made lids of all kinds. One of my jobs was loading the steel into the machines that would make the lids for the cans. I had six machines I was responsible for, and I loaded 16 tons of steel every eight hours.

I was enrolled in college and had a full-time job from 3:30 p.m. to midnight. I would go home and go to bed around 2 or 3 a.m. and try to get enough sleep to be able to attend my 8 a.m. classes. Sometimes, I would get to school early, sit in my car, and close my eyes. I would tell myself that I was just going to take a little nap. I would wake up only to realize that I had missed one or two classes. It did not help that many times I'd get off work late or end up working overtime hours.

Back then, we just did what we had to do. Taking out loans for education was unheard of. We worked hard and paid as we went.

I made the arrangements to gain an education, but I also needed to know what I wanted to study. What career was going to get me through life? One day, someone asked me what I had a passion for. I quickly responded that I liked to play around like I did when I was at the Boys Club. At that moment, it was like a light bulb went off in my head. I could make a career doing what I liked to do by earning a degree in physical education. I could teach school and coach. What a revelation!

In 1960, Betty and I got married while I was still in college. We visited various sites around Florida on our honeymoon. While in Fort Lauderdale, we saw a sign advertising round-trip airline tickets to the Bahamas for $35 each. We went back and forth. Should we go? Should we not go? Neither of us had ever flown before, so there was a lot of anxiety. Our answer was yes!

Wedding Photo – June 12, 1960

When we got inside the aircraft, it had web seating, and attendants came by to get our name for verification. As we were flying over the water, I remember us squeezing each other's hand, as the pilot announced we were going to be flying at 35,000 feet over the Atlantic Ocean and that in case of an emergency our life preservers were under our seats. However, no explanation was ever given as to how to use them. Gee! That was comforting.

As we landed in Nassau, Bahamas, we were greeted by a group of middle school boys selling alcoholic beverages. It was a shock to see these young boys, who appeared to be 12 or 13, peddling alcohol.

We decided to rent a car. At the time, Volkswagen Beetles were popular there. I asked the attendant if it had a full tank of gas, so we would not have to worry about running out of gas. He said he didn't know. There was no fuel gauge. He proceeded to light a match to look into the gas tank. Betty and I immediately did a 180 as fast as we could.

Anniversary photo, 47 years later, 2007.

In 1961, we had a daughter during my third year of college. Debbie was blonde-haired and blue-eyed. I continued to work at American Can Company, and Betty returned to work at the Merchants Association of Greater Tampa until the birth of our second daughter, Kimberly, in 1966. Betty decided she would go back to college and earn a degree to teach. This would make our working time more compatible. We would have the same work hours, school calendar, vacations, etc.

In 1962, I graduated with a Bachelor's in Physical Education and a minor in Middle School English. Students were required to have 15 hours of a language or take math classes to supplement. I was, and still am, decent at deciphering different elements and sources of prose, so I stuck with what I knew. I accumulated the additional hours in English, and it gave me enough hours to minor in it.

In August of 1962, I officially started my teaching and coaching career for a salary of $4,200 a year. I was hired at Buchanan Junior High School to teach PE and a study hall and to coach the boys' basketball team. However, I ended up being the head football coach and not the basketball coach. I also had no PE classes. Instead, I was given six middle school English classes and a study hall. It was a challenging time for me. Thank God for Betty. With her secretarial skills, she would help me every time she could. Two years prior, Betty had completed a two-year degree in Secretarial Science and began to work at the Merchants Association as an executive secretary. She loved that job dearly.

During my time at Buchanan, we were living in Port Tampa, and I was driving 28 miles one way to work. I had to start my days very early. I would leave home in the dark and come home in the dark. Betty worked until 5:30 or 6 p.m. and had occasional events in the evening, making our work times not very compatible. At that point, I could not wait to get a transfer to a school closer to home. I completed my internship at Monroe Junior High School under Roland

Acosta and Bill Turner. Both are now deceased. They took me under their wings and taught me a lot of what I know about coaching today. It was one of the most enjoyable years of my teaching career.

When Betty left her employment at the Merchants Association of Greater Tampa and went back to college to get her degree in education, we were solely dependent on my income. So, I did what most men would do. I got another job at the Boys Club. I drove the Boys Club bus to Port Tampa to pick up boys from that area. This gave them the opportunity to experience an indoor gymnasium, pool tables, ping-pong tables, and woodworking classes. There were lot of amenities for boys to entertain themselves.

While driving the bus one day, I got pulled over by law enforcement and was given three citations: one for no chauffeur's license, one for speeding, and one for reckless driving. As I was given a court date, I just knew that they were going to drop the hammer on me. I remember visiting with Stretch Murphy, the Boys Club director, and sharing my problem. He made a few phone calls.

I was instructed to dress nicely, get in line with the other offenders, and pay my dues. I knew that meant paying the ticket which would have been astronomical. I remember getting in line, and the fellow in front of me was given 30 days in jail.

When it was my turn, the judge read the offenses. I was guilty of having no chauffeur's license, speeding, and reckless driving. I was a first-time offender. The charges were dropped with the assurance that this will not happen again.

I told the judge, "Yes, sir. This will not happen again!"

On one occasion on the way back to Port Tampa, the Police Department blocked off Westshore and Interbay, the two streets that led in and out of Port Tampa. It seemed that something very serious had taken place. Later, we found out that one of the boys normally on the bus to go to the Boys Club did not go. Instead, he became extremely upset when a close friend of his was not allowed to come out and play. This young man climbed up on the porch of his friend's house, then climbed upstairs and stabbed the boy's mother to death. Things like that just did not happen in Port Tampa. Eventually, the young man was taken into custody and was incarcerated as a juvenile for a while. He did not serve a very long sentence.

Back in those days, Port Tampa was a "blue town", so distributers could sell alcohol on Sundays. The City of Tampa could not. This little town was quite popular on Sundays as there were several establishments that served alcohol. Not only did persons from outside the Port Tampa City limits come to purchase alcohol, but sailors from the oil tankers docked in Port Tampa, also visited the bars. Port Tampa also had its own police department and jail house during that time, and they were kept busy on Sundays.

Career at Monroe

Monroe
Middle
School

AFTER MY FIRST YEAR OF teaching at Buchanan, I was
able to officially transfer to Monroe Middle School. I
was at Monroe for seven years and had great success in all
my coaching endeavors. The school had 1,200 students. It
was basically wall-to-wall kids. All programs had to be well
organized in order to maximize time. There were three male
physical education teachers and three female physical education teachers. In the men's PE classes, each coach–Roland
Acosta, Billy Turner, and yours truly–would rotate jobs.

Herman – Coach at Monroe Junior High

We always averaged about 40 students per teacher. One teacher would stay inside and supervise the locker room. The other two coaches would meet the kids outside and line them up for mass calisthenics. We had a platform set up outside, and each coach took turns leading the drills. It was such a sight to see all the boys, in unison, doing their exercises. They were all in the uniform of red shorts and gray T-shirts. Then, the school was known as the Monroe Rebels.

The Power of the Tongue

One unique day, I remember when a young man came out late to drills and had on a different uniform.

I asked him, "What uniform are you wearing? Why aren't you in red shorts and a gray t-shirt?"

He replied, "I'm a new student. I don't have a uniform yet."

His T-shirt read, "Goose Bay."

I asked, "Is that your name?"

He responded, "No, it's where I was born–Goose Bay, Alaska."

So, I told him, "From now on, your name will be Goose Bay."

The name stuck. To this day, his grandchildren even call him by that horrible nickname. When I reflect back on it, all I can think is shame on me, shame on me, shame on me. Unfortunately, that was not the last time that I used words loosely.

As an adult and after teaching school for many years, I attended the wedding of one of my former students. It was an elaborate wedding. The reception was held at the Hyatt Regency Hotel in downtown Tampa. During the course of the evening, a young man, who was well-dressed in his tuxedo and a member of the wedding party, approached me. He was quite tall, and I wondered if he was someone who had played basketball for me.

The young man began to engage in a conversation with me and shared that he used to hate me. By then, I had been walking with the Lord for quite some time, and the idea of a former student hating me was very disturbing.

I responded, "Please tell me about it,"

He described, in vivid detail, an incident that occurred in the locker room at Monroe.

The particular incident he was referring to was during the year the school was filled to capacity. Approximately 120 boys would be in the locker room changing into their PE uniforms. Some boys at that age are very modest and would go to the restroom to change clothes in a private cubbyhole or the commode area.

As I was chasing boys out, I went into the restroom area and said, "You guys need to hurry up. Get outside! You're acting like a bunch of sissies."

That very word, sissy, was synonymous with being girly. It so deeply offended this young man that he harbored that hurt for years. I asked for his forgiveness and made no attempt to justify my actions because I knew they were wrong. He immediately forgave me, and I will always be grateful for that. It also taught me a great lesson about the power of the tongue. One word can lift someone up or destroy them. A word from a teacher is quite powerful, especially one from an assistant principal or principal.

For me, it was a lesson about being careless with my words, especially as a leader. I could cause damage. A simple word can alter someone's perception of who you really are. I had known that in theory, but it was now being demonstrated before my very eyes. I wish I had learned this during my early teaching years, so I did not continue to make that mistake.

On the flip side, another young man sought me out after his graduating high school. I was not in school that particular day. I had been laid up with a sciatic nerve problem in my leg that kept me from even walking. I laid on the couch in the living room. My wife, Betty, would leave the door unlocked, so I would not have to get up in the event someone came to the door. Sure enough, someone knocked at the door.

I said, "Come in."

It took me a moment to recognize the young man and for him to greet me as Coach.

He said, "I tried to find your home, and I was having a hard time. I noticed all the trophies on a shelf visible through a window to the outside. I figured Coach must be living here or maybe someone who might know where he lives."

The young man shared with me how that when his dad was in Vietnam, I was the only influential male figure in his life and how my words of encouragement got him through those very difficult times. He continued to shower me with blessings about how much I had done for him and how grateful he was. I've never forgotten that day.

Once again, the Lord showed me the power of the tongue. By your words, you are justified. By your words, you are condemned. We have a choice to speak life or death, to preach hatred or love. I was grateful that He gave me a win after having such a defeat as mentioned earlier.

Marine Corps Physical Fitness Program

One of the things I strived to achieve at Monroe was to get the school involved in the Marine Corps Physical Fitness Program. I contacted the officer in charge of the Marine Base Gym located on Gandy Boulevard to see what we needed to do. The Marines were most cooperative and came to the school to share their test program. The plan was to implement the program, and they would come back to administer the tests to see if we qualified.

It was a vigorous program that involved pull-ups, sit ups, push-ups, and a shuttle run that was all timed. We practiced until the kids were pros at it. On a given day, the Marines came in their dress blues and distributed the awards.

At the high school level, a Marine Corps Physical Fitness National Competition was held in Washington, D.C. Remarkably, two of our former Monroe boys went on to compete at the national level. One of the young men even ended up being a National Champion! This turned out to be quite the honor!

During track season, I was tasked to develop a track team to compete at the junior high level. If you gave a boy a choice between running track and playing baseball, he would choose baseball every time. There are enormous physical demands of track, and baseball is much more fun. So, I implemented a very creative program to combat that and to create an interest in track. In this program, students had their track practice mainly during the school day in physical education classes. Hurdles were practiced after school. As we got closer to competition, the team would start practicing the baton exchanges for relays. For my long-distance runners, I would train them with combat boots, only to take them off for the event. It doubled their endurance and reduced the fatigue during the event, allowing them to run faster for longer. For my long jumpers, I would place a hurdle right in front of where they would take off, so they would get the necessary height. They ended up converting that height into distance.

Most coaches strive to win an event with an overall average score. I focused on areas that required high skills. For example, every school has a kid who can throw the shotput. Not everyone has someone who can throw the discus. Throwing the discus requires a great deal of skill versus the strength of a throw. So, coaches would typically put the strongest kid in both events and expect him to excel in shotput and gain an average score in discus. Hurdles require lots of coaching and lots of skills, as does pole vaulting. Those participants were typically expected to earn an average score to even out the other events. For my team, I hoped to place at least three kids in each event in which they specialized. I was okay with a combination of third, fourth, and fifth place or first, third or even seventh place in that event. The point was to beat out an overall average score with one or two outstanding scores. With this strategy, we were County Champions several times. I was able to figure out the track meet scores within one or two points during the meets, and I could adjust accordingly on the fly.

Herman J. Valdes

COACH

The kids on the track team were tough, the days hotter than hot, the practice exhausting—and then there was Coach...

When I attended public schools in Tampa, Florida, there were few people in the Hillsborough County education system who knew anything about deafness, and they never seemed to be working in the schools I attended. Nonetheless, I was fortunate to have a few teachers and coaches who tactfully reminded me that being deaf was not going to excuse me from engaging in academic and athletic competition. My English teachers would give me fits about punctuation. I had to have three broken legs for a coach to excuse me from running track.

This story is about one of those coaches.

The world I grew up in was complete with religiously manicured baseball diamonds, fresh-painted asphalt tracks, and a few hundred South Tampa sports fanatics. South Tampa expected all of its school teams to win every single athletic endeavor.

Tampa is basically a baseball town. The managers of two 1990 World Series teams, Lou Pinella and Tony LaRussa, were both from Tampa. Dwight Gordon, pitcher for the New York Mets, and Wade Boggs, third baseman for the Boston Red Sox, were also part of Tampa's contribution to major-league baseball. Tampa produced a few NFL football players too—Morris LaGrande and Larry Smith, to name a couple. And pro wrestlers such as Dick Slater, a.k.a. Sergeant Slaughter. Tampa's most famous professional athlete ever is Terry Bollea, otherwise known as Hulk Hogan.

✰✰✰✰✰✰✰✰✰

To fulfill my neighborhood obligations while avoiding a bent nose, I played baseball on various fields of dreams for 9 years. My performance, at best, was mediocre. As an outfielder, I could catch a fly ball, chase down grounders and make pitchers miserable while trying to steal second. In football, I quit the first time Harry Hughes knocked me out. Forget basketball. Everyone is South Tampa hated basketball.

Baseball may still be the object of my middle-age fantasies, but track was the sport where I earned a few bars on my letter jacket and perhaps impressed a couple of girls enough to risk a date with me. I never achieved any spectacular feats in track, but it provided me with a wealth of important experiences that would have an eternal effect on my life.

Coach knew that I had a weakness for Cokes, especially after running 2 hours on the 100°-plus sun-baked Florida earth. He also had a psychological diagram of controls and switches on every other team member.

Everyone's first experience in any personal, athletic, or professional endeavor is an important one. My first experience with track was my first track coach, Herman Valdez. Coach Valdez was more concerned with how fast I ran, rather than how little I could hear.

I was in Tampa last year for a work-related meeting. It had been 5 years since my last visit. When the meeting ended, I drove across town to visit some friends for the weekend. My current home is a landlocked mental wasteland called Wisconsin. It's the kind of place cheeseheads can be entertained by watching their lawns grow—or watching paint dry on the wall. With the breeze from the Gulf and 3 cups of Cuban coffee, I was in seventh heaven just being in Tampa.

While driving down McDill Avenue, I recalled that Coach Herman Valdez, track coach extraordinaire, was now a principal at a school I was about to pass. 25 years had passed since Coach Valdez drilled us into dehydrated delusion at Monroe Junior High.

✰✰✰✰✰✰✰✰✰

The Monroe Junior High Track Team was comprised of a bunch of streetwise, scheming, tough kids from working-class homes. During the school day, we spent more time priming our teachers for placement in mental detention centers than concentrating on trivial things like academic development. Our attitudes changed drastically when it was time for track practice. Coach Valdez didn't take no shit from nobody!

Excellence in track requires a good oxygen depth or enhancing your ability to sprint the last 100 yards of a mile run although you feel as if you'd rather be in a coffin. Increasing oxygen depth or stamina calls for a strict interval training program. On an easy day this would consist of running 220 yards 10 times at a 30-second pace, 100 yards 20 times at a 12-second pace, and perhaps a 440-yard dash under 60 seconds.

I had blown my wind one day running the 220's faster than I should have. Coach walked over to me, grabbed my arm to ensure I paid attention, then said, "Bo, if you win this last 220 dash, I'll buy you a Coke."

Being the number-two sprinter, I would have to beat Davis Floyd, who was then the prime sprinter on the team. The other person in my sprint group was Morris LaGrande, who later went on to play for the Tampa Bay Bucs in the NFL. In 1967, Morris was 13 years old and definitely not the huge power runner he became with the Bucs. He was number three by an inch and always gave me a hard race.

Coach knew that I had a weakness for Cokes, especially after running 2 hours on the 100°-plus sun-baked Florida earth. He also had a psychological diagram of controls and switches on every other team member. How else would we have won the regional and conference track titles that year? For my want of a cold Coke, Davis and Morris never had a chance.

Coach Valdez saw immediately that my deafness was not going to interfere with competing and achieving the team goals. He was always generous with praise when we accomplished impossible aerobic feats

and tore our tails apart when we screwed up. With all the rough times adolescent 13- and 14-year-old boys endure in South Tampa, a nice comment from Coach was akin to winning an Olympic Gold Medal.

Following the Hillsborough Conference Track Meet, where I somehow managed to broad-jump 20 feet and 6 inches (which was one inch behind Morris), Coach was giving us a post-meet lecture. I was sulking and depressed about jumping so far and not being in first place. Fortunately, Coach was always easy to lipread. I enjoyed watching him talk and absorbed most of what he was saying.

Coach was letting everyone know how pleased he was, then turned directly towards me. "Bo, you might not hear me, but you did a damned good job!" It was the first time he made reference to my hearing impairment.

☆☆☆☆☆☆☆☆☆

As I drove the car into the school parking lot, I began having reservations about dropping by without any notice. Besides, after 22 years, he might not remember me. I parked the car, ambled into the administrative offices, then told the secretary who I was (I used my real name). She escorted me back to the principal's office where Coach currently works.

"Bo!" he exclaimed while giving me a warm hug that could

defuse the Iraqi crisis. I always know I'm in Tampa when someone starts calling me Bo. Principal or not, it was the same old Coach with the same old magic. Did he remember me well? He remembers everyone!

Coach wanted to know if I still had the newspaper article and picture of the 1967 Monroe Junior High Track Team. Of course I do. It is one of the few pictures I have of the old South Tampa Gang. We were practically undefeated that year. Undefeated because Herman Valdez was coach.

VINCENT HOLMES

Vincent Holmes became deaf at the age of 5 after contracting German measles. He grew up in Tampa, where he was mainstreamed in public schools.

A 1974 graduate of Gallaudet University, Holmes also holds a Master's degree in Rehabilitation Counseling. He has worked as a vocational rehabilitation counselor in Atlanta, Georgia, and is currently the State Coordinator of Services to the Deaf with the Wisconsin Division of Vocational Rehabilitation. He is a former president of the Georgia Association of the Deaf and a former member of the NAD Board of Directors.

Holmes has contributed a chapter to a forthcoming book, **Bright Silence**, about the experiences of mainstreamed deaf people. His interview with journalist Henry Kisor was featured in our September 1990 issue, and a humorous account of his visit to Chicago for that interview ("What are Those 'Pigs' Outdoors?") in our November issue.

Article from DEAF LIFE magazine, January 1991, written by Vincent Holmes, one of my former students.

We didn't have weights or a weight room at Monroe, so we made our own weights. We used buckets filled with concrete and a pipe in the middle. We tried to come close to 100 pounds. We built an obstacle course out of telephone poles that had been donated. I had parents and teachers bring chainsaws. We worked and were able to cut the logs and to make hurdles and balance beams. We also used the logs for training like the Navy SEALS. By squad, we would do curls with the log. We would do overhead presses with the log, pressing the log over our heads from right shoulder to left shoulder.

My statement to every boy and girl I coached was simple. "We will be the best conditioned team around."

We had homeroom track meets. Each homeroom had to participate. No one was exempt. Each boy or girl could choose three events: two in running and one in field or two in field and one in running.

I also had a track meet with my physical education classes. They never went head-to-head. They never competed person-to-person, only against the stopwatch. For example, I would take the times of the boys that ran the 100 and post the top three. I would do the same with the next period class and so on. With this, I was able to encourage many kids to come out and participate to be part of the track team.

Track became so popular at Monroe that we had nearly 100 students participating, all without having a track at the school. We sold donuts and raised money through a variety of means, in an attempt to raise the funds to build a track.

One day, I put on my coat and tie, went to our County Commissioner's office, and presented him with an opportunity to assist Monroe by building an asphalt track with seven lanes. I don't remember what the cost was at the time, only that it was sizable. The Commissioner agreed. It wasn't long before the County came out, and the track became a reality.

Shortly after the track was built, we found that some people were driving cars on it. Of course, the hot summers caused the asphalt to get very soft. We were concerned that the weight of the cars would damage the track. I went back to the County Commissioner and explained the problem that we had and that we needed a fence built around the track. Scriptures are clear. You have not because you ask not. The County assisted us again, by putting a fence around the track.

The next thing we needed was electrical and water hookups at the track; electrical to announce the track meet and water to meet the needs of the boys and girls participating. To accomplish this, the coaches, some faculty members, and even the principal participated in digging a trench from the locker room all the way out to the track to install the wiring and the plumbing. The track stands to this day. We were so pleased to have accomplished that task.

Monroe Junior High football team, 1968

Monroe's football team was second to none. We ran a pro-style and wide-open offense. At that level of coaching, my biggest thrill was when we played against Madison Junior High. Their quarterback was John Reeves. He eventually went on to stardom at Robinson High School and the University of Florida, and he played professional football. At the time, the coach at Madison was Ray Escobar. Ray was my history teacher in junior high school and was the first teacher to paddle me in junior high school.

Coach Escobar had the best quarterback in the city and supposedly the best junior high football team in the city. I did my homework and devised a great game plan. We won the coin toss and elected to receive. We planned a double reverse on the kickoff return. Our student, Bruce Sparling, had tremendous speed. We wanted him to end up with the ball. He did, and we scored on the opening kickoff.

On the kickoff after the touchdown, Madison fumbled the ball, and we recovered. Our next play from scrimmage was a halfback pass, and it went for a touchdown. The score was 14 to nothing. Ray Escobar got very impatient. He would run John Reeves to the right and to the left and have him throw the ball. It was all about John Reeves. So, we focused on John Reeves and won the game 14 to 13. Sadly, John Reeves recently passed on to be with the Lord.

While at Monroe, I ran a summer recreational program for first through ninth grade. Each morning, the students would follow an assigned schedule. After lunch, they would choose the activities in which they wanted to participate, almost like electives. In the afternoons, we offered all kinds of activities. Every day, kids went swimming and took swimming lessons if they wanted to.

As the children were waiting in line to board the bus for swim lessons one day, a young boy was just wailing. He was crying so hard that it caught my attention even though I was indoors. I came out to check and see what was going on. I asked, "What's the problem?"

I thought the boy had been harmed in some way.

With tears streaming down his face, the young boy said, "I swallowed my dime."

I reached in my pocket, grabbed a dime, and gave it to the boy. He immediately stopped crying. Problem solved.

On another occasion at the end of the day, I noticed a young boy standing at the corner of the building next to the downspout of a gutter system.

I inquired, "Why are you still here?"

He said, "I'm stuck."

As I looked at him, I noticed that he had slid his knee in behind the downspout.

I said, "Well, I guess we'll just have to cut your leg off."

Oh my gosh! That was the wrong thing to say. He began to let out bloodcurdling screams.

"I am just joking. We aren't going to cut your leg off."

He was surely stuck. I tried picking him up and sliding him up and down, knowing that what goes in must come out. All my tactics failed, so I had to get an aluminum bat and pry loose the straps that held the downspout in place. In fact, the straps came undone, and I was able to free him. In my attempt to be funny, I had traumatized this young boy.

Many of Monroe's students from the Port Tampa area loved to fish. I was constantly being invited to join them.

One evening, they said, "Coach, you have to come fishing. We are catching some huge snook by the Shell Oil dock."

I decided I would join them that evening. I parked my car, grabbed my rod and reel, and made one cast. My lure hit the side of a ship that was anchored and began to sink slowly. A huge snook grabbed my lure. I landed the fish, and it weighed over 20 pounds.

After I showed the boys, I said, "I'll see you all in school tomorrow."

It was fun to see the surprised look on their faces. With just one cast and one huge fish, the Lord was shining on me that evening!

Would you believe I also coached swimming while at Monroe? At the time, we didn't even have access to a swimming pool, but one of our students was an avid swimmer. His dad was the Base Commander at MacDill Air Force Base. The boy's father arranged for us to practice at the pool on Base. So, I went on a quest to put together a swim team.

During that time, the powerhouse of junior high swimming was Wilson Junior High, located in the Hyde Park area. Monroe swam in three meets that year, and many of our swimmers' times qualified to enter the city- swim meet. Being a rookie coach to the swimming community, I was disappointed to learn that we did not swim in enough meets to qualify entering the city-wide swim meet. The truth is that with the few boys I had I felt they might have placed highly had they been afforded the opportunity to participate. It was not meant to be.

While I was serving my tenure at Monroe, we experienced the county-wide teacher strike. Teachers were striking, not just for more pay but for more supplies, better facilities, and better conditions. I will give you a small example. I coached every sport–swimming, football, basketball, and track. The yearly supplement was just $300.

I was passionate. We needed to get the attention of the parents, the administration, the general public, and the taxpayers in the community. One day, many of us walked out, and the classroom teaching positions were immediately filled with anyone they could find to cover the classes. Not knowing how long the strike would last, I proceeded to find a part-time job.

New homes were being built behind Monroe. I walked over and asked the contractor if he had any job openings. He did, and I spent some hot days putting down roofing shingles. While on the roof, I could observe what was going on at the school with my students and the school's equipment. Some had no interest in taking care of the facilities or the equipment. They were just looking for a paycheck.

Many administrators and coaches lost their positions due to the walk out.

I had a co-worker and close friend. He was like a brother to me. In his search for a larger salary, he resigned as a teacher and became an insurance agent with a major insurance company. He eventually sold me a product in the form of whole life insurance.

Several years passed, and I received communication from the insurance company asking me for the payments on a loan that I had supposedly taken out on my insurance.

I responded, "I'm sorry. I don't know what you're talking about. I have not taken out a loan."

As I try to chronologically recall the events, I remember my friend telling me that a check had been inadvertently written. If I would just sign it, he would deposit it back into my insurance account. However, he was actually depositing the check in his own bank account, hence the reason the insurance company called me about the loan.

Around the same time, I was changing insurance agents to a highly recommended individual. He went to seek out my funds to transfer them to the new company. He found that I had no money left in my account and alerted me. It was about this same time that I got the letter from my insurance company inquiring about the loan payment. It was then that I realized something was definitely wrong.

Betty and I reviewed all of our records and conferred with our new insurance agent to make certain that everything was as he said it was. I had one recourse to correct the situation. I was going to do it according to the Bible. If you have ought against your brother, go to your brother and share with him. If he does not believe you, meet with him again and bring a witness (Matthew 18:15).

So, I made a phone call, and I laid it all down. I remember the individual asked for forgiveness and recognized that he had done some stupid things in order to have some cash on hand for a sure investment opportunity he had come across.

Here is the truth. If he had asked for the money, I probably would have loaned it to him at no interest. As I recall, the total amount taken from my insurance policy was in excess of $12,000.

After I listened to his explanation, I said, "There are two things you must do, or the letter that I have prepared to be sent to the State Insurance Commissioner will go in the mail immediately."

I relayed my conditions. He must tell his wife and family what he had done, and he must tell his employer. I gave him a deadline and asked him to call me to let me know that he had done what he had been asked to do. I remember it was near Christmas, and we that we had actually met and talked prior to the ultimatum that I had given him.

The deadline was up, and I did not hear from him. So, I called him. Again, He pleaded for forgiveness. He knew he had done something very wrong. On that same day, I kept my word. I sent the letter with documentation to the insurance commissioner, and they began an investigation. It was revealed that the individual had been forging my signature on checks and depositing them in his account.

I ended up going to court on his behalf and shared with the judge that this was a good man and a good father who had made a serious mistake. Scripture is very clear. If you forgive little, little will be forgiven you. When he once again asked me for forgiveness, I truly forgave him. To this day, we still have a strong relationship. This individual has gone on to be redeemed and has prospered, all with a solid relationship with our Lord and Savior and his family.

We have an advocate with Jesus Christ, our Lord and Savior. When he comes into your life and totally reconstructs you, forgiveness takes on a new meaning. I thank Jesus Christ for filling me with enough love that I could forgive unconditionally. I could not have done that prior to my salvation.

Career at Robinson High

T.R. Robinson
High Shcool

ONE OF THE THINGS I wanted more than anything in my professional career was to go to Robinson High School and coach football. I started my career as a football coach. I coached every sport Monroe had, but my favorite and most successful was football. I let it be known that I would like to be considered for the first available football coaching position at Robinson.

In August of 1969 and after six years at Monroe, I was offered a position at Robinson. I served as a physical education teacher, junior varsity football coach, scout for the varsity football team, and varsity basketball coach.

When I went to Robinson, several of my former students came along. I coached several in the seventh, eight, and ninth grades. Now, I had these same students as sophomores. As you can see, I ended up having some of those individuals for six out of their 12-year educational experience.

There were some great athletes. One was Morris James Legrand. Morris had a brother by the name of James Morris Legrand. This caused a great deal of confusion at the state level because they thought we were trying to play a student longer than his eligibility called for. Morris was a star in every sport he played. During one basketball season, he was missing from practice. I inquired as to what was happening with him. Some of the boys told me that he was sick at home. I decided to pay a visit. I found a very sick boy with a high fever. There was no thermometer in the house and no medication to lower the fever. I did what any good parent, coach, or teacher would do. I went to the drugstore, bought a thermometer and some aspirin, went back to the house, put a wet compress on his forehead, and stayed until the fever subsided.

Otis Rogers was another great athlete with whom I was very close. I took this young man fishing numerous times. I also took him crabbing and cast netting. On one occasion, I took him offshore fishing for kingfish. We were anchored up and chumming for the kingfish, also known as king mackerel. I needed to loosen the anchor rope. His middle name was David. I always called him by that.

I said, "David, let out some anchor rope."

David went to the bow of the boat and let out some rope. After a few minutes, I noticed the boat was drifting.

I said, "David, did you tie it off?"

His response was, "You didn't ask me to tie it off. You just said to let out some rope."

David had not noticed that the anchor rope was not tied off. I lost 150 feet of anchor rope, eight feet of anchor chain, and the anchor. That was quite an expensive outing.

On another occasion when we were fishing offshore, David was looking kind of grayish. I knew it was the beginning of seasickness, so I proceeded to play a joke on him. I took some squid and placed it between two slices of bread, as if I were going to make a sandwich and eat it. That's all it took. David was over the side, vomiting his guts out. He could not wait to get back to shore.

One time, David and I went crabbing–Florida style. We took a number-two washtub, a gas-operated Coleman lantern, and two crab nets. We waded out into the creek.

I said to David, "You really need to be on the lookout. Sometimes, water moccasins are out."

That was a mistake. I could hardly turn to my right or left without stepping on David. As we proceeded walking and looking for blue crabs, a mullet jumped out of the water and hit David right in the chest. I think David walked on water all the way back to shore.

David graduated from Robinson High School and accepted a football scholarship to attend the University of Tampa, playing for Coach Earl Bruce. Later, Earl Bruce was hired at Ohio State, and he took David with him. David was later drafted by NFL to, I believe, the Chicago Bears. However, he did not make the cut, though he came ever so close.

Talking with David about this experience, he shared with me that he was playing weakside linebacker and trying to cover halfbacks coming out of the backfield. That was like a mission impossible for David. Hence, he came home and began to live a normal life.

David was in the hospital the last time I saw him. He had a form of cancer. The time of diagnosis to the time of his passing was just a short while. When I went to Tampa General Hospital to visit David, his brother, Rusty, was in the room with another friend. I wanted to make sure that David knew Jesus Christ as his Lord and Savior, so I led the entire room in a prayer of salvation. With all my heart, I believe that when David took his last breath that he was in the presence of the Lord.

I knew David's family well. They loved me, and I loved them. That is true to this day. When I run into his sister, Jackie, or his brother, we reminisce and hug. Jackie was a great athlete in her own right, destined to be a Division I volleyball player. Other circumstances came into her life, and that did not materialize.

I invented some creative discipline involving David's family. Before David passed away, I became the principal of Monroe Middle School. Jackie had a son there. He got into some difficult times behaviorally, and I was at my wits end. I called Jackie and told her that I was going to try one last intervention with her son, or I was going to have to suspend him for 10 days, pending a change of placement. Suddenly, I got this bright idea. I decided to call the young man's Uncle David and seek his assistance.

I told the young man, "I'm going to call your Uncle David."

Very arrogantly, he replied, "You don't know my uncle."

I took out my phone and called David. He picked up the phone, and we started a conversation.

"David, I need to see you at school. Can you and Rusty come over?"

He said, "Of course, Coach. We'll be right there."

When they arrived, I had David, Rusty, and this troubled young man in my office.

I addressed the young man, "Here's my intervention. I want you to edge the track. Since I can't turn you loose with an edger that's gas-operated, I am going to give you this hand edger to use."

I turned to David and Rusty and said, "I will need one of you to sit out there and supervise."

So, David and Rusty took turns supervising. When the young man was finished, he came to the office to inform me that he was done.

I said, "Well, let's go inspect your job."

There we were–David, Rusty, this young man, and me.

I said, "You only edged the inside of the track. I want the outside of the track edged as well. Then, your punishment will be complete."

They returned to the track, and the young man satisfactorily completed the assignment. Thus, he was able to remain in school.

Coaching at Robinson

Prior to my first basketball season at Robinson, I was quite successful as a junior varsity football coach. Along with Coach Lou Garcia, we gave Robinson's junior varsity its first undefeated season. Football reigned supreme at Robinson. They had pregame meals, game day shirts, pep rallies, and all sorts of recognition.

Basketball was the stepchild that I had inherited. We practiced outdoors and at the Marine Base Gym on Gandy Boulevard. Our home court for games was at Plant High School. That first season, I lost 18 straight games. The newspaper would read "Valdes loses another one." I realized that the general public and the press did not know the agreement that I had with the principal. Basketball was not highly regarded at Robinson during that time.

Robinson High School had no gymnasium. Even though I had played the game and had successfully coached the game at the junior high level, I believed that if I did everything that I had done at Monroe that I could achieve instant success at the varsity high school level.

It was not until the end of that first season that I won four straight games. I then realized I had to become a basketball coach. By most standards, I became a pretty good one. I never had a losing season again. I went on to experience many, many successes and accolades, especially when Robinson got its gymnasium. We would win 15 and lose one, win 10 and lose 10, and win 18 and lose five. Most coaches would have killed for those kinds of records. I wasn't satisfied.

I read every book I could get my hands on, books on skills and drills. I read John Wooden's book, "They Call Me Coach." Coach Wooden was the legendary basketball wizard of UCLA, who won 11 National Championships. I watched films after every basketball game until the wee hours of the morning to plan the next day's practice. Each year, I attended many clinics to see what the rest of the basketball community was doing.

During my time at Robinson, Henry, a student athlete, approached me.

"Coach, get me a pair of shoes, and I will play varsity for you."

I told Henry, "Buy your own shoes and try out like anyone else."

Needless to say, Henry did not show up for basketball that season.

The following year, he came to me and said, "Coach, get me a pair of shoes, and I will play varsity for you."

Again, I said, "Henry, you've missed the whole season. You're a year behind. Buy your shoes and try out for the junior varsity program. If you do well, I will move you up to varsity."

He did just that. When he played junior varsity, his friends and the spectators gave him such a difficult time that he quit.

The following year, Henry returned.

"Coach, I'm going to buy my shoes. I want you to give me an opportunity to play for you."

I gave him that opportunity. It was a defining moment in Henry's life, as he became a starter on the varsity basketball team. I also helped him get a scholarship to Edward Waters College. Many years later, Henry had a daughter. She attended Ballast Point Elementary School. My wife, Betty, taught fourth grade there. I was thrilled to get reacquainted with Henry and his family.

One night when Robinson played Hillsborough High School at Hillsborough, the gymnasium was full. At the beginning of my coaching career, there were certain goals that I had set to achieve. One was to defeat Hillsborough High School in basketball.

I always told the kids, "We can win. I know we can win. We are better than they are."

That particular game started with the two officials lining up the players going in the wrong direction for the jump ball. At the time, neither one of the coaches, myself or Frank Vining, noticed this error. Hillsborough scored three baskets. Robinson scored three. Then, Robinson scored a fourth time. It was then that the coaches got the attention of the officials to acknowledge the error.

The rule states that to correct an error it must be done before the next live ball. The three baskets scored by each team prior to Robinson's fourth basket would stand because they were already on the board before the error was corrected. The last basket Robinson High School scored was taken off the board because the error was corrected before the next live ball. This meant the score was still tied. Now, we settled in for a very emotional and heated rivalry.

I had used all of my timeouts, but I needed to stop the game to talk to the kids. Jack Frost – yes, that is not an error and is his name – was one of the officials. Unlike today where we have three officials, we only had two then. Jack was administering a free throw at the far end of the court, away from Robinson's bench.

I cinched up my tie and walked from my bench to the opposite basket to see if I could get a technical foul to thereby stop the game and give me time to talk to my players. When I reached the official, who was about to give the ball to the shooter to shoot his free throws, the official turned and looked at me.

He said, "What are you doing here?"

Meanwhile, the crowd was going crazy! They wanted the officials to throw me out, screaming for a technical foul.

I said, "I know I can't be here. I need to stop the game. I thought if I walked out here that you could give me a technical and that would stop the game."

I didn't win that game, but my idea and my intentions were right. You don't need to throw a chair like Bobby Knight, coach of the University of Indiana, did in a tournament in the Bahamas, curse an official, or threaten an official to get his attention. Walking out on the court was not such a bad idea after all, and I used this technique several more times during my career.

The 180 – My Conversion Experience

In October of 1975, I was invited to a men's retreat in Leesburg, Florida. A good friend, Ron Waldo, had invited me each year, and I always found an excuse not to go.

This time, he said, "I've bought your ticket, and you have to go."

So, I packed my rod and reel, my swimsuit, and my tennis racket. I was going to this men's retreat to enjoy the lake and the recreational facility that was there. That night was a defining night for the rest of my life.

The speaker was the Dean at Oral Roberts University. His topic came from the third chapter of Revelations.

"To the angel of the church in Laodicea write: These are the words of the Amen, the faithful and true witness, the ruler of God's creation. I know your deeds, that you are neither cold nor hot. I wish that you were either one or the other! So, because you are lukewarm–neither hot nor cold I am about to spit you out of my mouth." (Revelations 3:14-16 NIV).

This described me. Translated into Latin, the word spit, or spew, literally means to vomit. On Sunday, I am in church with my family. After practice on Thursdays, I'm in the local tavern with the macho coaches. I would repeat this week after week. During that conference, I prayed that God would make me the man he wanted me to be, the husband he wanted me to be, the father he wanted me to be, and the coach he wanted me to be. I wanted Him to make me whatever He wanted me to be.

There was no music or no calculated invitation, just a nudging of the Holy Spirit. I accepted Christ into my life and asked Him to forgive me of all my sins.

"That if you, confess with your mouth, "Jesus is Lord," and believe in your heart that God raised him from the dead, you will be saved." (Romans 10:9 NIV)

The Word also says that when you ask Jesus to come into your heart that your name is written in the Lamb's Book of Life. That evening, I called Betty at home and told her that I had made a very sober decision. I had accepted Christ into my life and asked Him to make me the man that He wanted me to be.

After returning from the men's retreat, the following Sunday was Layman Sunday. The head pastor of our church was at a retreat for pastors, so the associate pastor conducted the service. He arranged for some of us to give a short summary of our experience at the men's retreat.

When it was my turn, I gave an emotional testimony. While I may not have been so eloquent, I shared my heart.

"If you do not have certainty that if you cross the street after church and get hit by a truck that you would go to Heaven and are not secure in your heart, you need to come forward and accept Jesus Christ as your Lord and Savior."

Then, I called for some music. The choir sang one verse of "Just as I Am, Without One Plea." No one responded. So, I asked that the song continue. Still, no one responded. On the third time, there was a response. My family came forward and knelt at the altar. Others began to come down. Before long, the altar was full. Do you know what? I didn't know what to do with them. What was sad was that the associate pastor didn't know what to do with them either.

As I look back on this, it was the beginning of the boldness to share Christ with others. The Lord began to show me that this could be done in a more suave and loving manner. I became more involved in Sunday school and Monday night home groups. I can look back on this today and share that the true church is like the Church of the Apostles which was in the homes.

I immediately started coaching differently. I was no longer verbally abusive or as physically aggressive. I treated the players as if they were my own sons. My fellow coaches at Robinson wanted to know what was going on with me. They felt I had become a religious fanatic. I shared that if it were fanaticism that it would wear off. If it didn't wear off, they would know it was for real.

Each game day, the basketball team had a pregame meal. Then, the team would come over to our house. Betty welcomed the boys with open arms. The boys even called her mom. She would later say that the biggest expense we had during those days was for toilet paper, as the boys used a lot of it before leaving for the games. I would do a short devotional to share the Gospel, the Good News, with the boys, and we would then leave for the game.

Filled with the Spirit

It was also during this time that my wife and I grew the most spiritually, along with other families. We did many things together. Monday night meetings were held at the home of John and Mary Charlotte Counter. They had three children. We had three. There were also other similarities. As a result of these home meetings, the introduction of the Holy Spirit became a serious topic.

Every Sunday morning, a beloved lady, Audrey Schaefer, would ask me, "Are your spirit-filled yet?"

To this question, I would answer, "I think so."

She responded, "If you just think so, you're not."

Over a period of time, the Lord showed me the scripture of Luke 11:11-13.

*"Which of you fathers, if your son asks for a fish,
will give him a snake instead? Or if he asks for an
egg will give him a scorpion? If you then, though
you are evil, know how to give good gifts to your
children, how much more will your Father in
heaven give the Holy Spirit to those who ask him?"*

One evening during a prayer time by myself, I asked for the infilling of the Holy Spirit. I couldn't wait for Sunday, for I knew that Audrey Schaefer was once again going to ask me if I was spirit-filled. Mrs. Schaefer was true to her calling, and she did.

That time, my response was, "Yes, I am!"

Her rebuttal was, "How do you know?"

"In Luke 11:11-13 of God's Word, it states that if I but ask for the infilling of the Holy Spirit that I will have it," I said.

She answered, "Now, you have it."

Those were special times. I was able to lead many of the boys and girls and a few adults along the way to Christ. Some even ended up in the ministry. God honored my commitment.

Darrell Dawkins

When I was an athlete in junior high and high school, my dad was rarely around to watch me participate. Years after I accepted Christ and had my life going in the right direction, he did not miss a basketball game.

The 1975 State Basketball Finals were held in Jacksonville in front of 10,000 fans. I was 35.

I asked myself, "What am I doing here?"

It was our style to send our boys to shake the opposing coach's hand. It was my way of intimidating the other coach. However, the opposing coach sent one person, a player, to shake our hands. That person was Darrell Dawkins.

Darrell was 6' 11" and a monster of a man and a player. I am grateful that dunking was not allowed back then. Our game plan was to focus on the other four players and keep their scoring down. We knew that Darrell was going to get his points. However, it was the other two guys that we did not count that just lit it up.

As we were coming home from Jacksonville after being defeated by Darrell Dawkins and the Orlando Evans team, Alvin Holder came over and sat next to me.

He said, "My little brother is going to bring you back to State, Coach."

True to his word, Charlie Bradley was on the scene five years later.

While having lunch with the faculty after the Orlando Evans game, I was asked, "How good was Darrell Dawkins?"

I proceeded to tell them that he was good, but it was the other two guys that killed us. About that time, I lost all my credibility as a basketball coach.

One teacher said, "Did you read the paper? Darrell Dawkins just signed for $1 million with the Philadelphia 76ers."

Darrell Dawkins was the first person in the NBA to sign right out of high school. There was one other individual, but he was in the ABA league. I believe it was Moses Malone.

Sadly, Darrell Dawkins just recently passed away.

1975 Season

Our 1975 season ended with those State Finals in Jacksonville. To this day, I can say that team was probably the best basketball team that I've had in all my years of coaching. We had size. We had quickness. We had jumping ability. We had confidence. In the middle of all that, we now had God. Many of the boys had accepted Christ as their Lord and Savior. Some of their lives were difficult. Some had a great deal of difficulty even into their adulthood. Most of their stories had a good ending. Some are now working with other boys, teaching and coaching basketball. Their drug habits have been overcome, and they have become productive adults in our community.

I still have a good relationship with these individuals. Whenever we meet, we hug and talk. I cherish those moments, the crowd's respect, and all that went with it. For 10 years, Robinson Basketball was highly regarded as one of the finest programs in the State of Florida, and I received many accolades.

If you remember, it was my goal to make Robinson basketball as good as Robinson football. This was accomplished, and we were truly a stronger program than the football program. I've had numerous players from those teams play at major colleges. Three played at Florida State – Herb Allen, Alvin Holder, and Murray Brown. Clarence James played at Tulane University. Jimmy Martin played at Jacksonville University and Charlie Bradley at University of South Florida.

Transformation On and Off the Court

One night during a Plant City basketball game at Robinson High School, an altercation took place on the court. Both coaches ran out to break it up. It was a little chaotic for a moment, and I turned around and bumped into my dad.

I said, "You can't be out on the court."

His feelings were hurt. For the next few games, he refused to sit right behind me. Instead, he sat four or five bleacher seats up from me. Eventually, he worked his way back down to his seat of honor and became the team chaplain. I coveted that relationship.

Many people from our church began to support the Robinson team and attend all of the home games. After those games, we would make a giant circle in the middle of the court, join hands, and ask the basketball fans to please honor or join with us in prayer. Dad or I would lead the prayer. During this time, I couldn't get enough of the Word. I was constantly listening to the Bible on tape with a headset and an old-fashioned tape player.

Coaching Girls' Volleyball

Around the time that Robinson High School got a new gym, Title IX was about to take place. Equal rights for women in sports was introduced, and girls' volleyball was being implemented. I felt that if I could become the girls' volleyball coach that I would have better control of the gym. It was so. I was appointed the girls' varsity volleyball coach. At the time, I knew little to nothing about volleyball, other than we used to play "jungle ball." I read every book I could get my hands on, and I attended several clinics. I knew that I could reach kids and motivate them.

The team became the first Western Conference Volleyball Champions in Hillsborough County Public Schools. We didn't even have proper uniforms. The girls wore basketball tank tops and shorts. I motivated these girls to be the best they could be. They would even run up the bleachers to chase volleyballs.

I remember the girls saying to me, "You have to coach us just like you do the boys."

I responded, "If I do, you won't stay around. You will quit."

I did coach them like the boys. I demanded the same, if not more, from them than I did from the boys.

Basketball season and volleyball season overlapped. On given days, my boys' basketball team would practice first, and the girls would have the late session. While the boys were wrapping things up, the girls would put the net up and begin their warm-up drills.

On the next day, volleyball practice would be first. While I was wrapping things up, the boys would take down the net for the girls. Two years later, we were State Champions in volleyball. The volleyball team had the game ball bronzed and placed on a pedestal type of display. The names of all the players and the coaches were engraved on the award.

Exactly 20 years later, my daughter, Melanie Humenansky, who was the volleyball coach at Bayshore Christian School at that time, won her first State Championship. It was one of three more to come. I took the trophy from my State Championship and presented it to Melanie and her girls with their names engraved on the opposite side of the Robinson Championship team display.

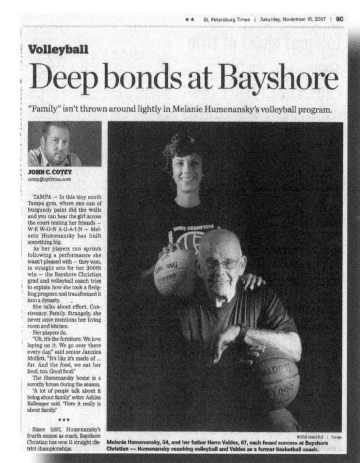

St. Petersburg Times | Saturday, November 10, 2007 | 9C

Volleyball

Deep bonds at Bayshore

"Family" isn't thrown around lightly in Melanie Humenansky's volleyball program.

JOHN C. COTEY
cotey@sptimes.com

TAMPA — In this tiny south Tampa gym, where one can of burgundy paint did the walls and you can hear the girl across the court texting her friends — W-E W-O-N A-G-A-I-N — Melanie Humenansky has built something big.

As her players run sprints following a performance she wasn't pleased with — they won, in straight sets for her 300th win — the Bayshore Christian grad and volleyball coach tries to explain how she took a fledgling program and transformed it into a dynasty.

She talks about effort. Consistency. Family. Strangely, she never once mentions her living room and kitchen.

Her players do.

"Oh, it's the furniture. We love laying on it. We go over there every day," said senior Jannica Mollett. "It's like it's made of ... fur. And the food, we eat her food, too. Good food."

The Humenansky home is a sorority house during the season.

"A lot of people talk about it being about family," setter Ashlea Ballengee said. "Here it really is about family."

• • •

Since 1997, Humenansky's fourth season as coach, Bayshore Christian has won 11 straight district championships.

ROSS MANTLE | Times

Melanie Humenansky, 34, and her father Herm Valdes, 67, each found success at Bayshore Christian — Humenansky coaching volleyball and Valdes as a former basketball coach.

St. Petersburg Times volleyball article

Fellowship of Christian Athletes

I had numerous girls playing volleyball at Clemson, Florida State, and many junior colleges. If you sponsored a club at Robinson, you didn't have to do bus duty. So, I volunteered for the Fellowship of Christian Athletes. As mentioned earlier, one reason I wanted to be the volleyball coach was to have full control of the gym and the practice times for volleyball and basketball. Later, I pondered as to whether my motives in sponsoring the club had been skewed.

The Fellowship of Christian Athletes met twice a month in the auditorium. I'll never forget the first meeting. I asked approximately 100 students to raise their hands if they were a Christian. Some did. So, I asked the others what they were. Some said Baptist. Some said Catholic. Some said Lutherans. Do you get the picture? So, we embarked on a journey to share Jesus Christ with as many students as we could reach.

On one occasion that I thank God was the only occasion, I witnessed and was involved in a deliverance ministry. Keep in mind that I had not been walking with the Lord for very long at that point, and I was still learning an awful lot. I guess this was the Lord showing me that there is power in the name of Jesus.

On a caravan to a Jesus Festival in Orlando, I was pulling a camper trailer. Someone else was driving my father-in-law's motorhome, and we also had a pop-up camper. I had a young man, who I will call LB, with me. LB was a football player at our high school. He was so strong. He could bench press 350 pounds. At this point in his life, LB had been caught up in experimenting with drugs. As we drove up Interstate 4, I asked him what his expectations were at this Jesus Festival.

He responded, "I need to be delivered from drugs."

At that point, I think I changed the subject. Once we were all set up in a sort of circular wagon-train formation, I invited LB to join me with some of our chaperones, who were very mature Christians. As we sat in one of the campers, LB shared his problem with drugs.

There was a prayer for deliverance, but there were no manifestations at that time. We went about the business of getting our campsite set up. God's word is faithful and true, and the prayers of those chaperones went forth. God heard the prayers and was about to deliver LB from his drug problem.

During the keynote speaker's presentation later that day, the speaker stopped and said, "There is someone in the audience that has been delivered from drugs even as I speak."

I nudged LB and said, "Buddy, that's you."

The evangelist said, "You need to come up and receive your healing."

LB made his way to the stage. There were people there to greet him and asked him why he was there.

He responded, "I'm the one who has been delivered from drugs."

As LB walked towards the evangelist, the evangelist raised his hands, never touching LB. LB was slain in the Spirit. This massive human being, who could bench press 350 pounds, was lying on the stage. LB got up, took a few more steps, and went down again. The evangelist prayed for LB, and we all praised God for LB's deliverance.

There was more to come. As LB wobbled off the stage, his legs were like jelly. He took his seat next to me.

I asked him, "What just took place?"

He responded, "I've been set free."

I had Melanie, my youngest daughter, sitting on my lap. My wife was next to me. LB was to my left, and all the other members of the Fellowship of Christian Athletes were sitting in the row in front of us or on the same row where my family and I were.

All of a sudden, the power of God was so strong that the whole row we were sitting in went over backwards. The power of God just pushed us over. It was as if God had just walked in front of us, and we could not stand or sit.

What I am fixing to share with you is a testimony. It is something that I witnessed and experienced and not something someone shared with me. LB was on the floor on his back, wriggling almost like a snake. I put my hand on his chest and began to pray. He began to reach for my throat. He began to utter words that I have never ever heard. Meanwhile, there seemed to be utter chaos in the auditorium.

Well-meaning brothers in Christ were screaming, "Satan, get out of him! Satan, leave him alone!"

I knew enough to ask my wife and several of the chaperones to take all of the other kids outside. We were almost 30 strong in terms of our group. I recall kneeling over LB with my hand on his chest and praying. Someone reached down and tapped me on the shoulder. As I looked up, there was a young man. He appeared to be in excess of six feet tall with red hair and green eyes.

He said to me, "He doesn't belong to you. He belongs to us."

Several of the young men who were with us tried to reason with this individual. He stood up and began to take swings with his fists at two of our boys. For some reason, he could not hit them. Eventually, he was escorted out, and we never saw him again. By this time, LB was totally calm and coherent.

The first thing out of his mouth was, "I want to be baptized."

There was a makeshift swimming pool for baptisms. LB was escorted there by some of our students. Someone was under his right arm, and someone was under his left arm, as LB was still very wobbly. That day, LB was baptized and became a new creation.

When we got back to school, we would recognize LB's speech when it was his thoughts and his vocabulary. When the Spirit of God began to speak through him, it was evident that it was not LB. Everyone would just look at each other with a big smile on their face. I'd like to tell you that this was a major success story; however, there is scripture that says where an evil spirit leaves that seven more deadly move in (Matthew 12:45). That was the case with LB.

I had no knowledge or teaching of a deliverance ministry. I did not know how to best proceed to help LB. What he needed was to be disciplined, taught, and embraced with the Word of God. I learned from that experience. Unless someone who has been delivered is willing to be discipled or that the person involved with the deliverance is able to disciple the individual, one should not be part of a deliverance ministry. I learned a mighty, mighty lesson.

Many years later, LB visited me at Monroe Middle School. I was the principal at that time, and I was delighted to hear that LB was once again on the right path. He was attending church and Bible studies. His life was in order. The Spirit of God was now feeding him. LB had gone on to the military. As a civilian after serving his four years, he became a paramedic based on his training in the Armed Forces.

Shortly after his visit, I learned that LB had died. He was driving on the interstate, stopped to assist in an automobile accident, and gave mouth-to-mouth resuscitation to an injured person. It just so happened that the injured individual had Hepatitis C. LB contracted it, and that is what eventually killed him. I thank God that LB's name was written in the Lamb's Book of Life.

* * *

At this point, I would like to share another story. Those members of the FCA who desired to do so met in our home every Wednesday evening for a Bible study and a time of socializing. During one of those meetings, the captain of the volleyball team, Terri Lynn Martin, was off to the side looking kind of sad. She was a precious girl I loved dearly.

I went up to her and asked, "Terri, what's going on?"

She proceeded to tell me that she did not have a date for grad night or the prom and was feeling kind of left out.

I brought Betty over, so we could pray for a mate for Terri. I said, "Let's get real silly with God. How tall do you want this guy to be? Of course, he should be a Christian. What would you like him to look like?"

We wrote all these things down, and Terri kept the list with her. Within six months, she met a young man, Mike Fordham, who would become her husband.

Mike was a student at Bayshore Christian School and graduated at the same time Terri graduated from Robinson. Terri went to Florida Southern. Mike went to Southeastern University. They went on a mission trip together. Shortly thereafter, they were married. Terri became a special education teacher, and Mike became a Methodist minister.

Many years later, Terri's life was cut short. She had flu-like symptoms and went to the ER. They sent her home thinking it was nothing major, but her condition worsened. Within days, she passed away. I attended her funeral and was able to share her love story with those in attendance.

While at Florida State University visiting my grandson, Michael, I was introduced to one of Terri's daughters. I had a chance to share this story with her. She shed tears of joy, learning of her mom's love story. Sometime later, she found the original paper where Terri had written all the criteria she was seeking in a mate. To this day, I have the list.

❈ ❈ ❈

On another occasion, we had our Fellowship of Christian Athletes meeting at Indian Rocks Beach at the home of one of our parents. At the conclusion of the evening, we made our prayer circle. We had a little routine. I would pray first. When I finished, I would squeeze the hand of the person to my left, and it would be their turn to pray.

This night, we had a young man, who often stuttered, in the midst of our circle. When he did, it was pretty bad. Someone in the circle prayed for that young man's stuttering to go away. When it was the young man's turn to pray, it was very evident that God had taken away his stuttering. We all had our heads bowed and were joined by hand. When we heard him pray without stuttering, all heads came straight up.

Someone said, "You're not stuttering."

Tears began to flow, and hugs were everywhere. God had just revealed Himself to us in a powerful way.

❄ ❄ ❄

On another occasion, I was transporting the girls' volleyball team in the back of my truck on the way home from a game. I had a Ford F150 pickup truck with a white topper and a vinyl boot between the topper and the cab. This allowed the air conditioning to flow from the cab to the back of the truck. On the corner of Kennedy and North Boulevard, I stopped for a traffic light.

At the corner, a homeless person was lying on a bench. I pulled off to the side, gave some money to two of the FCA girls, and asked them to go into a sports bar restaurant on the site and buy a sandwich, a drink, and some chips to give to the man. I told them to tell him that the Lord God loves him. They did just that, and we proceeded on.

At a wedding many years later, one of those girls approached me.

She said, "Coach, you won't believe what I just did. I just purchased that restaurant on the corner of Kennedy and North Boulevard."

❄ ❄ ❄

The Fellowship of Christian Athletes did a lot of good work at Robinson. One family hit a rough spot. Their refrigerator wasn't working, and there was no food in the house. On hearing this, some of the students went out, located a refrigerator, and put it in the house. They also bought groceries. They did all this without the family knowing. It was such a joy to see the family's response. The Lord was honoring their newfound commitment.

✽ ✽ ✽

One of the fondest moments of my career was to watch a Florida State versus Tulane basketball game. Two of my former players, Murray Brown and Clarence James, were competing against each other. Both boys wore number 34. As I watched the game from my couch, I reminisced about how good God had been to me to allow me to see the fruits of my labor.

✽ ✽ ✽

While at Robinson, one of my players, Charlie Bradley, was being recruited by and wanted to attend Florida State University. That was his first choice. His second choice was the University of Florida. These are very big decisions for a 17-year-old to make. Because Charlie's half-brother, Alvin Holder, and Herb Allen had a difficult time at Florida State, Charlie's mother felt more comfortable keeping Charlie in town. Therefore, Charlie, otherwise known as CB, signed a letter of intent with the University of South Florida.

CB didn't feel comfortable and was not at peace with his early letter of intent signing. His practices were sluggish, and it appeared that something was wrong.

I met with CB and said to him, "You really are uncertain about the letter of intent that you signed, aren't you?"

CB replied, "Yes, Coach."

I knew that we could not have a championship season unless our leading scorer put forth his best effort. This situation had put Charlie in a depressed mood.

I asked him, "Do you want me to make this right?"

Charlie nodded his head to the affirmative, so I called his mom and explained to her that we needed to focus on our current season and not have any distractions. She agreed and gave me permission to visit Coach Lee Rose at South Florida. I made an appointment, put on my shirt and tie, and walked up to Lee Rose's office.

Keep in mind that I'd already had another player, Lewis Shepherd, at South Florida. Lewis played the post and did a good job for them. During the time they were recruiting Charlie, I sat in the Rose Garden. After this meeting, I had a feeling I was moving to the nosebleed section.

When I met with Coach Rose, I sat in front of him. There was a big desk between us. I shared with him the conversation between CB's mom and myself. His response was quite ugly.

He said, "All you want to do is ride Charlie's coattail and sell him to the highest bidder."

He was implying that I was seeking a job at the college level by riding Charlie's coattail and somehow influencing Charlie's signing.

As I stood up and leaned over his desk, I said, "Coach, I've been here long before you got here. I'll be here long after you're gone. You see – I have had other players that went to other universities. In fact, I have been offered a position as an assistant at one of those universities."

I continued, "So, you see, Coach Rose. I don't need to ride Charlie's coattail. By the way, you can destroy Charlie's letter of intent, as we are going to focus on our current season. When it's completed, I'm sure Charlie will discuss with you your offer of a scholarship."

I adjusted my tie, turned my back to Coach Rose, and walked out. I no longer sat in the Rose Garden. My inclination on the move to the nosebleed section came true. As it was, Charlie did sign with South Florida.

"Cuda" Patterson was Charlie's best friend, a Robinson graduate, and a good basketball player. He signed with Florida College. In his second year, Florida College became National Junior College Champions. Cuda was the main reason they were able to achieve their success.

Charlie became the all-time leading scorer at South Florida. For two years, he tried to convince Lee Rose that he needed to sign Cuda. Had he done that earlier, Coach Rose would have had immediate success. Charlie and Cuda had played basketball together since junior high school.

People in the community have tried comparing Herb Allen to Charlie Bradley. I say that Herb's game was way ahead of his time. He was doing things with such skill that people called him "Hotdog" or "Showboat." I saw Herb as someone who needed to be put in a position in our offense where he would be able to create and use those talents. Herb also played defense with a passion and was very self-confident.

Charlie was a finesse player, an accurate shooter, and a strong rebounder. He lacked the thickness of his body and a strong desire to be as good defensively as he was offensively.

Both players led their teams to the State Finals. In 1975, Herb Allen's team faced the giant Darrell Dawkins of Orlando Evans. In 1980, Charlie Bradley's team lost by two points to Pensacola Washington. Both teams ended up as State Runner-Up. It's very difficult and unfair to try to compare the two players and their teams when opponents are different. Each had his own uniqueness and strength.

Today, Charlie Bradley works with the City of Tampa's Recreation Department. He loves the Lord and his family.

Academically, Herb didn't feel like he needed to go to class or to take the books seriously while in college. His life went spiraling out of control, but we serve a big, big God. Today, Herb loves Jesus with all his heart. He has committed his life to working with young boys and girls, so they might not go through the difficult times like he did. We do serve a God of many beginnings, and a God who loves us immensely. He gave us His only Son, Jesus, that whosoever believes in Him should not perish but have eternal life (John 3:16).

❊ ❊ ❊

One Robinson game in particular, stands out. It was the game that led us to the Final Four. The Robinson Knights played the Lakeland Dreadnoughts for the opportunity to go back to the State Finals. We had been to the State Finals in 1975. It was now 1980. Just like Alvin Holder had predicted, Charlie Bradley was going to lead us back to State.

There was an overflow crowd for the game. The principal did not even get in the gym. If we won, we would head to State. If we lost, we would have been defeated by a very good team. We had an undefeated season up to that point. Now, we were going to play Lakeland again. This time on our court. They had a team that was ranked as high as third in the nation. They had several High School All-Americans: Alonzo Allen, Tim Strawbridge, and Wayne Peace, a guard. Peace later became the quarterback for the University of Florida football team.

Kids in the apartments across from the Robinson gym were scalping tickets. There was literally no space for even one more person to sit. All the hype of the previous year was now in place. With 17 seconds left in the game, Robinson High School found itself seven points down. People were leaving the gym. News reporters were calling in the score.

God had a plan.

I called timeout under the basket at the east side of the gym. I ran an inbounds play that I called "The Box." It became a three-point play. Now, Robinson was only down four points, and the clock had not moved. We put together a full-court press.

Back then, the five-second count would continue as long as the ball was in the air. Lakeland threw a long pass down the court. The count was 1, 2, 3, 4, and then 5. A five-second count was called. It was now our ball under our basket again, and the clock still had not moved. We ran the same identical play, made the basket, and Cuda got fouled.

Cuda was the nickname that the boys gave him because he was as quick as a barracuda. His basket was good. Because he had been fouled, he was now shooting a free throw.

He looked at me and said, "Don't worry, Coach. I've got this."

I just wanted to just smack him and then hug him. He made the free throw. There was still seven seconds on the clock. Lakeland inbounded the ball. We were down one point and were forced to foul. Lakeland had not missed a free throw all night. They were 17 for 17 and made the front end of the one and one. They missed the second shot. We rebounded and ran our fast break to the baseline. Tim Wheelis took a left-handed jumper and missed.

Sylvester James grabbed the rebound and tried to stuff it, but the ball hit the back of the rim. As it was coming off the rim, Charlie Bradley grabbed it and stuffed it at the buzzer. We won 69 to 68. The jubilation in the gym was incredible. It was breathtaking. It was a tribute to God, and we gave God all the glory.

Robinson Gym Dedication – L-R John Edwards, Brian Peterson and Charlie Bradley with Coach Valdes

Spare Time

In addition to coaching, I still managed to go fishing, usually on a Saturday or Sunday afternoon. On this one occasion, my grandson, Matthew, and I were launching our boat, and it was cold. There was a man at the boat ramp offering to help launch and dock boats. For that, people would give him cigarettes or beer.

After fishing hours later, we got back to the boat ramp. The man was still there, assisting boaters by tying off their boats. Matthew and I put our boat on the trailer and went home. I could not get this guy off my mind. It was cold, and he didn't even have a jacket. So, I decided that I needed to give him my expensive Robinson letterman's jacket which was very warm.

When we arrived back at the boat ramp, I located him and asked what his name was.

He replied, "Pancho Villa."

I'm certain that this was not his name, but that's how he identified himself.

I asked, "Where are you staying?'

"I live under that bridge," he said.

I asked, "Which bridge?"

"That bridge over there," he replied, as he pointed to the Gandy Bridge.

I told Pancho that the Lord had told me that he should have this jacket.

He said, "Thank you."

Pancho reeked of alcohol. The day was getting darker, as the days are shorter in the wintertime.

I returned home. Once again, I could not get Pancho out of my mind. I wondered when was the last time he had eaten. My grandson and I stopped cleaning the boat and went to Burger King to buy hamburgers, fries, a milkshake, and a Coke. I was determined to feed Pancho.

As we reached the boat ramp, some of my Robinson students were having a beer party. As I approached, they scattered, as they should have. I looked for Pancho and noticed that he was sitting on the ground, leaning back on the tire of an automobile that had a boat trailer attached. I guess the owner of the vehicle was still fishing. We walked over towards him. He looked as though he were dead.

I reached down and shook him. I told him that I had brought him some food.

He looked up at me and began singing, "Everybody loves somebody sometime."

He repeated it several times.

I went home again. I finished cleaning my boat. It was dark. I still couldn't get Pancho off my mind. I called my buddy, Bob Lewis, and asked if he would go with me to take Pancho to a detox center. There, Pancho would have food and a warm place to stay.

We talked Pancho into going with us, so he would have a place to sober up and get a meal and a roof over his head, even if it were temporary. As we arrived at the detox center, they confiscated his belt and his shoelaces. They searched him for any weapons.

As I walked with Pancho to the area where he was going to sleep, several other residents of the detox center began to reach out, grab my hand, and ask me to pray for them. I did.

One man grabbed me and asked, "You're Coach Valdes. Aren't you?"

"Yes, I am," I replied.

He began to tell me that he played basketball for Chamberlain High School. He played against my team and mentioned that Robinson had won. I didn't remember that game or who won or lost. At the time, I was doing God's work just by listening to his story.

Career at Bayshore

Bayshore
Christian
School

I N 1982, PASTOR BOB SHELLEY of Bayshore United Methodist Church, the church my family and I attended, approached me.

He said, "Herman, I believe you're supposed to be working here at Bayshore."

I responded, "Pastor, you can't afford me. Even if you could, why would I leave my brand-new gymnasium at Robinson and the best basketball program in the state of Florida?"

"Herman, if God is in it, it's going to happen," Bob said. "It would be a promotion."

I inquired, "What does that mean–more money?"

He said it could, but all promotions come from God. He quoted scripture from the book of Psalms. Pastor Shelley had planted a seed, and that seed would just continue to grow in my spirit.

Pastor Shelley and my father, Chico, went to Israel. They both prayed that I would someday be part of this ministry. Many years prior to this, some high-level administrators from Hillsborough County Public Schools would make occasional statements that I had a lot of leadership abilities. They believed that there was a place for me at the next level.

I always responded, "What does that mean?"

They were always very elusive, stating it could mean a number of things. It could mean becoming an assistant principal.

One day, I finished an appointment in downtown Tampa. Since I was already in the area and dressed in a coat and tie, I decided to call the Superintendent's office to see if he was available for an appointment. To my surprise, he was. He said he had a few minutes, and he would be happy to meet with me. I made my way to the school office building, went upstairs, greeted his secretary, and was ushered to Dr. Sheldon's office.

I said, "Dr. Sheldon, I know your time is valuable, and I won't keep you long. You have made some comments, along with some of your assistant superintendents, that you thought I had potential as a leader in the school system. What exactly did you mean by that?"

Dr. Sheldon was very noncommittal just like the other assistant superintendents.

His response went something like this, "Well, there are no guarantees. If an opportunity arises, I'll keep you in mind. Keep up the good work."

I knew at that moment that I was getting closer to saying yes to a position at Bayshore Christian School.

Bayshore's Principal, John Guedes, was a fine man and a hard worker. He was the most organized man I've ever met. The school needed a principal, and Bob Shelley asked John if he would accept the position.

John said, "I'll do whatever you need me to do."

John and his wife, Ann, had no children of their own. They had been missionaries for the larger part of their lives. There was nothing in their background that indicated they had any experience in the field of education and, more importantly, working with children. Yet, John became principal.

After my meeting with the Superintendent and a great deal of prayer and conversation with my precious bride, we decided that I would accept Pastor Bob Shelley's offer to join the ministry at Bayshore United Methodist Church. I had a great deal of knowledge about the school, having served on its School Board for several years. My position was assistant principal, athletic director, and basketball coach. I also dealt with all the discipline of students in grades six through 12.

I spent 20 years of my life teaching physical education, health, and some middle school English dressed in shorts and a T-shirt. Now, I was in a coat and tie, managing boys and girls, and assisting John Guedes in managing the school.

I also coached basketball. It made for a full day when you're the basketball coach and a school administrator. At the first basketball practice I conducted, several of the boys were very apprehensive. They didn't know what to expect from this Robinson High School coach, who had gone to the State Finals twice. Bayshore Christian School had not won 20 games in four years combined. In my first year, Bayshore celebrated 20 wins.

The players did not know how to respond. They needed to learn how to be winners. They needed to know how to act during a game. The fans needed to learn how to act during the game, especially now that we were winning. Pep rallies were something new. The principal did not know how to respond. I think he was just in awe of all that was transpiring with athletics at Bayshore.

God only knows how many mistakes I made that year and how much time I spent in prayer. God delivered me from all those mistakes.

"But God chose the foolish things of the world to shame the wise; God chose the weak things of the world to shame the strong. God chose the lowly things of this world, and the despised things- and the things that are not-to nullify the things that are, so that no one may boast before him." (1 Corinthians 1:27-29 NIV).

This verse was certainly me. I felt like Gideon. Remember when the angel came to visit him to tell him that he was going to be a leader of an army? All Gideon could say was that his clan was the weakest in Manasseh and that he was the least in his family. He was stating that he was the least of the least. He was exactly what God wanted, so no man could boast. I saw God's hand in all of it.

At the end of my first school year at Bayshore, we left on a family vacation. I remember saying something to Betty that my daughters probably overheard.

"I have made so many mistakes, and I have learned so much. Next year is going to be just wonderful."

While on the vacation, I got a phone call from John Guedes. He wanted to know when I was coming home. The school had a financial crisis, and John needed my assistance in trimming the athletic budget by $20,000.

I had no idea that there were plans in the works to dismiss John from the position of principal, and I was going to be offered that position. It actually had the appearance that I was brought from Robinson High School to replace John. That was so far from the truth.

On my return, I was visited by the head of Bayshore's School Board and was offered the position of principal.

I responded, "If it's between John and me, the answer is no. If you're telling me that John is gone whether I accept the position or not, the answer is yes. I will accept the position."

Just a year prior, I was in shorts and T-shirts. Now, I was the Head of School. The school needed stability and leadership. Everyone desired to be wanted and needed. Being able to do this is one of my strengths. It didn't take me very long to develop a healthy team.

I did place one condition on the School Board. They needed to have a meeting with the faculty and staff to explain why John was no longer the Head of School. Some had loyalties to John that I needed to win over.

I surrounded myself with three unbelievably loyal, dedicated, and strong Christians. Each were not afraid to work. Valentina Stevens eventually became the assistant principal and curriculum specialist. Mazie Young was the school secretary, and GeeGee Erickson was the elementary principal. When I met with these ladies, I asked them something specific.

"Can you be loyal to the ministry and loyal to me? Can you tell me what I need to hear and not what I want to hear?"

We made an incredible team.

My first quest as the Head of School was to seek accreditation for the school. I found out that the Florida Council of Independent Schools accredited Berkeley Prep, Tampa Prep, and the Academy of Holy Names. Immediately, Val Stevens began to inquire about the process to become accredited by FCIS.

Meanwhile, I felt that if I was to represent the school and associate with the elite that I needed to get my master's degree. My next endeavor was to visit the University of South Florida to apply for graduate school. I visited the registrar's office with my paperwork, and the interview began.

I was told, "Mr. Valdes, your high school grades were not all that strong, and your college grades, except for your last year, were not that strong either. On the national teacher's exam, you scored a 502, and the minimum required is 500. You barely made the requirement for the GRE exam that you just took."

After listening, I responded, "In college, I worked from 3:30 p.m. to midnight. I was a husband, a father, a full-time employee, and a full-time student. I am currently the head of a private Christian school. I have almost 25 years of teaching experience and administrative experience. All I need is an opportunity. Would you rather I take my money to St. Leo, Arizona, or one of the other online schools, or should I just play the minority card?"

The individual immediately sat back in her seat and said, "Mr. Valdes, we will be more than happy to grant you an opportunity."

I had already taken some graduate courses. Every time I needed to renew my teaching certificate, I took a class that I knew would count towards a master's degree. Now, I was the principal, the basketball coach, the husband, the father, and the graduate student. I got my Master of Educational Leadership with a 3.6 GPA.

Accreditation

It was now time to go through the accreditation process. FCIS sent a team out for three days. They fell in love with our school. They gave us high marks in many of the things that we were doing; however, one of the most important things was that our library was not up to par. For me, it was a defeat, and I do not handle defeat very well. I don't just curl up and sulk though.

The pastor at the time was Rev. Frank Seghers. He and I joined hands right on the spot where we needed to build a library and began to pray that somehow God would provide the finances needed to build the new library. Within a month and without me or anyone asking, this precious lady, Louise Ramey, wrote a check for $350,000.

I needed to learn how to build a library. I assumed that the first thing to do was to hire an architect, so we did. Unfortunately, we discovered the man was not a true Christian walking in faith and was involved in an inappropriate relationship. So, I confronted him and shared that he was either to repent and ask for forgiveness, or he could not be the one to build our library. He did neither. As a result, he was not the one to build our library.

Instead, we hired a member of the church, Seth Sandige. He was involved in construction projects across the community. We had architectural drawings and all sorts of plans that had been laid out. All of a sudden, I had this revelation. Hillsborough County Public Schools build libraries all the time. I made a phone call and learned that the lady I needed to talk to was Mary Jane Haven.

Mary agreed to assist Bayshore and practically adopted me. She took me to five or six libraries in the school system. She showed me what not to do and reminded me that media specialists needed to have the media center laid out in such a way that they could observe all that went on in the media center. After consulting with Mrs. Haven, changes in our plans had to be made, and another set of drawings were required.

We built a soundly constructed library with classrooms upstairs. The building is still functioning to this day. As the library was being built, Mrs. Haven called and asked what we were going to do about furniture–bookshelves, control counters, tables, chairs, and all the other pieces needed in a media center. I had not given it much thought yet. At that point, she asked me if I was interested in purchasing the equipment on bid through Hillsborough County Public Schools.

God's hand was in all this! A small, private Christian school purchasing all its furniture through the school system. Only God can do these things.

At the completion of our new library, it was now time to prepare for the next accreditation. These take place every five years. We could not wait to see what FCIS would have to say this time. We passed with flying colors and have passed with flying colors every five years since. Now, the school is also accredited by the Southern Association of Colleges and Schools which is recognized all over the United States.

The school had and still has a weekly chapel service, and Bible classes every day. I told all students taking Bible class that they weren't going to just take Bible class. They were going to pass Bible class. During this time, I often spoke in chapel. In my heart, I was driven to lead as many of these boys and girls to Christ as possible.

I don't know that we've ever really qualified the statement I'm going to make, but it appeared that almost 80% of the student body's families were not churched. The school is a big and wide-open mission field.

One conversion stands out to me. It was with Jack Myers, who now heads Jack Myers Ministries. This is an international ministry that shares the gospel around the world. While a student at Bayshore Christian School, Jack was saved at the altar at Bayshore United Methodist Church and was filled with the Holy Spirit. He began to speak in another language. Jack attests to this in several of the books he has written.

Fundraising

Another one of my Head of School responsibilities was to raise funds to offset the cost of tuition. Tuition at Bayshore has never covered the actual cost. The heads of many of our families were blue-collar workers. Of course, we also had many professionals. In order to keep tuition affordable, we had to raise funds.

One evening, my dad called me.

He said, "I believe that you need to have Colonel Oliver North as your guest speaker at your next fundraising banquet."

Twenty to 30 table hosts were needed to sponsor tables of 10 and invite others to attend as their guests. When I first started these programs, the cost per ticket was minimal. It was somewhere around $20 per person.

Dad had been watching the Christian television station, channel 22, and the guest that day was Col. Oliver North. He was a hot name during that particular time. He had just gone through Congressional hearings over some issues with the Iran Contra situation. You either liked him, or you didn't.

One thing I always wanted to do was to please my parents. I was always seeking their approval. When Dad called, I made all kinds of excuses.

I said, "Dad, how am I going to get in touch with this high-profile public figure?"

His response was, "Just figure it out, and do it."

I said, "Okay. If I call him and he answers the phone, I will know that God is in this, and I will proceed from there."

Wouldn't you know it? I called, and the person on the other side of the line responded.

"Oliver North, may help you?"

It took me a while to gather my thoughts, and I assumed that he might have thought that I had hung up.

I said, "Colonel, I am the head of a private Christian school in Tampa, Florida. We're having a large fundraising, auction-type dinner, and I would like to invite you to be our guest speaker."

He replied, "Tell me a little bit about your school."

I proceeded to share the highlights of our school, not wanting to take up too much of his time.

He said, "My fee is $5,000."

I said, "There is no way in the world that we could afford to pay that kind of money."

He wanted to know how much we could afford. While I don't remember the exact figure, I believe it was less than $1,500 plus accommodations. There was a pause on his end.

He said, "Well, if you can promote the sale of my book, *The Jericho Sanction,* at the banquet, I think that maybe we can make this work."

Col. Oliver North, guest speaker at BCS fundraising banquet.

I gave him the February date of the function, and we agreed on the time with more details to follow. I could see God's hand in this whole event.

I called Dad and said, "Dad, guess what? Oliver North will be our guest speaker at our next banquet."

We now had to determine the number of tables to secure, and the number of table hosts needed. Several days after my conversation with Oliver North, I got a phone call from an individual. This person questioned me about security for

Oliver North. Never in my wildest dreams did I even think of security.

I asked, "What does something like that cost?"

Again, God intervened.

The gentleman on the other line said, "Mr. Valdes, we do this for Col. North at no cost."

I said to myself, "Hallelujah! Hallelujah! Thank you, Jesus!"

During this time, we had a student at Bayshore Christian School whose father was the head of a church called The Avenger. This gentleman and his church leaned towards white supremacy and were very radical. However, he had the utmost respect for me because I would just tell him what I expected from his child and what I expected from him as a parent. When I mentioned this individual to the security detail, they assured me that this situation would be taken care of during the event. They would actually monitor him, as they knew where he lived and had security in that neighborhood.

We secured the Hyatt Regency on the Courtney Campbell Causeway. This facility allowed us to seat several hundred people. In my mind, I wanted the Marine Corps Color Guard, military presence from MacDill Air Force Base and from the Marine Amphibious Base on Gandy Boulevard, some City Council members, the Mayor of Tampa, and other dignitaries in attendance.

My next step was to call the Base Commander at the Marine Amphibious Base. I explained to him that I would love to have the color guard present the colors to kick off the evening. Of course, I mentioned that Col. Oliver North was our guest speaker. I was just name dropping.

His response shocked me.

He said, "What makes you think that we would do anything for Oliver North?"

So, I responded as usual, "Sir, who is your supervisor?"

Another gentleman came on. I believe his position was second-in-command. I explained my request for the color guard to him and that the prior individual had told me there was no way they would do anything for Oliver North.

This gentleman said, "Mr. Valdes, we will do anything in our power to make that evening special."

They agreed to march in, four abreast. I was good with that until I started looking at the facilities a little closer. I realized that if they marched four across that I would lose almost five tables. Once again, I called the Base. The same individual I had first talked to on my prior call picked up the phone. I explained to him that it was nearly impossible for us to have the color guard come in four abreast. He insisted the best they could do was to march in four across. I once again asked to speak to his superior. I explained to this gentleman that the facilities would work best if they could march in single file.

He replied, "Mr. Valdes, we will come in however you want us to come in."

Next, I approached my basketball team and asked them if they would be ushers for this event. Of course, they said they would. I went to a local tuxedo rental place and asked the proprietor if he would like to participate in this event by donating tuxedos for my ushers. I assured him that we would give his firm credit in our program. He agreed, and I took the boys to the shop. They all tried on their tuxes to make sure they fit. Of course, they wore tennis shoes with the tuxedos on the night of the event.

One of my daughters, Kimberly, has experience in marketing. She wanted to know how much press I had rounded up and how I planned to use the press. She suggested that I create a press pass, so the press would only come in by invitation.

To increase fundraising, we developed a certain level of contribution that allowed guests to have their picture taken with Oliver North. Oliver North's book was used as centerpieces for the tables. In fact, we placed two books at each table.

During this time, my dad was struggling with emphysema and was pretty much limited to a wheelchair. Dad's desire was to meet and greet Oliver North. I asked Oliver North about transportation to Tampa. An alumnus from the University of Alabama was going to fly him to Tampa in a private plane. On the day of the banquet, I met Col. North at the airport, introduced myself, and shook his hand.

He was on the move and said, "What time do you want me back?"

I gave him a time–5:30 p.m. We had sold over 60 tables at 10 individuals per table. We expected a full house that included all the dignitaries that I mentioned before. If you can, envision me all dressed up in my tux. My dad was in his wheelchair with an oxygen bottle strapped to the side. We were at the curb waiting for the arrival of Oliver North.

Our meeting time came and went. Six o'clock came and went. The press wanted to know where Oliver North was. He had a lot of security that were supposed to keep an eye on him.

Finally, Oliver North arrived in a yellow taxicab.

I asked, "Where have you been?"

He said, "Well, I went to the Hyatt. I guess I didn't realize there were two Hyatt Regency hotels in Tampa."

He said he realized he was at the wrong place when he saw all these pirates with cutlasses and muskets They were in full costume, and all painted with makeup. This function was in February. If you have lived in Tampa, you know that this is the time of the Gasparilla pirate invasion.

Having arrived late, Col. North was now in a hurry to change clothes.

He said, "Follow me. I want to hear some more about the school before I speak."

I believe his assistant had his bag with his clothing. We were now in the men's restroom. He was changing clothes while learning about Bayshore Christian School. You really cannot make this stuff up. This really happened. When

Oliver North spoke that evening, you would have thought he had known the school from its inception. He was incredible and had such command and presence. The evening was a great success.

We didn't raise as much money as we had hoped, but we had a full house. Now, many people, who had never heard of Bayshore Christian School, had an idea of where the school was located and what the mission was. It gave the school great exposure. The exposure and, of course, the experience was worth the entire evening, and I will never forget it.

I would like to mention that my bride was there with me every step of the way. None of the things I have been involved with would have occurred without her support and the support of my beautiful daughters and my father.

* * *

Six months after the date of that banquet, I got a phone call from Chico.

"Hey, who's going to be the guest speaker at your next fundraiser?"

I replied, "I haven't thought that far ahead."

Dad said, "James Irwin, the astronaut, is a Christian. Call him. He needs to be your guest speaker."

So, you know what I did.

I told Dad, "I'm going to call. If Col. Irwin picks up the phone, I will know that God is in this."

I know it's kind of hard to believe, but James Irwin, who was living in Colorado at the time, answered the phone. I explained to him why I had called, and he graciously agreed to be our guest speaker.

Betty and I had the opportunity to sit with Col. Irwin and have him share some of the highlights of his being in orbit and in a state of weightlessness. We also learned he was an avid skier. He wrote a book, *In Search of Noah's Ark*. I recommend it to anyone who is intrigued by the story of the ark. Once again, we had an awesome banquet, and Col. Irwin was a major hit.

I don't know what I was expecting when I first met Col. Irwin. I thought he would be a little taller. He explained, however, that if he were taller that he would not have fit in the space capsule. He shared that many astronauts suffer from heart disease and bone density issues later in their life.

* * *

Once again, Chico was on target. For the next banquet, I jokingly told him that I was going to get Oral Roberts to come down and speak to us.

Chico responded, "I think that's a great idea."

I called Oral Roberts University, spoke to Mr. Roberts' secretary, to Mr. Roberts himself, and made the arrangements. The Hyatt Regency Hotel in downtown Tampa has a presidential suite that can be accessed by driving your car into an elevator. The car and its occupants are taken directly to the presidential suite. It's all about security.

Oral Roberts arrived a day early, and we had planned a sit-down dinner with Mr. Roberts and the School Board members. John Counter was the Chairman of the School Board at that time. John and I proceeded to send out invitations to all School Board members, the pastor, and some of the staff. This started as a wonderful evening but ended with some hurt feelings.

A good friend and a strong school supporter, who was also a School Board member, was inadvertently omitted from the list and was not present at the dinner. Upon learning of this omission, it seemed like the damage was done, and the relationship was not the same ever again–no matter how much we apologized and asked for forgiveness.

That function was also a big success. During that time, Oral Roberts was at the top of his television programs and speaking tours. He shared with me that to have a successful fundraiser dinner you need to start on time and finish on time. If you didn't finish on time and dragged on, every minute was going to cost you money. I understood what he meant, and we followed a strict timeline.

Power of Prayer

During those days as Bayshore Christian School's Head of School, I was invited to numerous events and conferences. One of these events was at Camp Florida in Brandon. There was a gathering of numerous pastors, preachers, and evangelists. I was not only new to this group, but I was also new at these types of gatherings. At this conference, a discussion was held to figure out what we were going to do about a horrible drought that had lowered the lake to a level more than anyone could remember. I could not believe how long the discussion went back and forth and back and forth.

I felt led to raise my hand and suggest we should send a corporate prayer to God. You do know that when a person suggests something that it almost always means that they are the one called upon to get it done. True to form, it was suggested that I should be the one to lead them in prayer for rain, so I prayed what I thought was a passionate prayer.

Later that afternoon and after the conference was over, it began to rain, and it rained for approximately one week. Each day, there was a downpour. I received a call from a friend of mine, Bob Lewis, who had been at the conference. Bob wanted to know if I thought we should now pray for the rain to subside.

At that same conference, I felt led to go to the altar to have the elders and some prominent preachers pray for my new journey as the Head of Bayshore Christian School and to lay hands on me. I remember I was dressed in a nice suit with a crisp shirt and a dazzling tie. As I knelt, these men placed their hands upon me for my new task at hand. I began to laugh. It was not really a Holy Ghost laugh. I was laughing because when I was kneeling I noticed the holes in my shoes were visible to the audience.

This conference was on a Saturday. The next morning in our Sunday school class led by Dallas Albritton, members were asked if there were any prayer needs or if anyone had something to share. I raised my hand and shared about my experience at the altar with holes in my shoes.

As I finished sharing about my experience, Dallas Albritton began taking up an offering. I thought this was the usual Sunday school offering. When the collection was completed, Mr. Albritton presented me with the offering plate and the contents. He proceeded to share with the Sunday school class that he thought it would be all right if the class blessed me with a new pair of shoes.

Other people were coming in to attend church, and they were watching me take money out of the offering plate and put it in my pocket. I thought to myself – I wonder what those people are thinking. They probably thought that I had no shame. Sometimes, we have to recognize that God can be very humorous as we serve him.

At that same Camp Florida conference, my friend and brother in Christ, Bob Lewis, had been complaining of hemorrhoids. I suggested that he anoint his hemorrhoids with oil and told him I would be praying for his healing. I did tell him that I was not going to lay hands on them. In less than a week, Mr. Lewis testified that his hemorrhoids had shrunk and disappeared, and he wanted to thank me for my prayers.

It doesn't matter how silly the world may look at some of the things we do. If we are genuine, we can rely on Jesus Christ for all of our needs and all of our healings. Certainly praying for hemorrhoids to shrink and disappear is okay.

On another occasion when I was presiding over chapel at Bayshore Christian School, I needed to pray for my newborn grandson, Matthew. At some point during the chapel, word had come to me that Matthew was diagnosed with jaundice.

I did not know that many babies are born with jaundice. I went to the altar and began to weep hysterically.

GeeGee Erickson laid hands on me and prayed for me.

She whispered in my ear, "It's okay. This is not uncommon. This is not a life-threatening situation."

Over the years, those in attendance at that Chapel remind me of the day that I went to the altar and wept for my grandson.

Chapel and Spiritual Emphasis Week

Once a year, we have a Spiritual Emphasis Week, now called Spiritual Enrichment Week, at Bayshore Christian School. During this week, we would have chapel twice a day for the high school students. On Friday, our main chapel culminated the previous four days. The youth pastor of our church made all the arrangements for a guest speaker in the afternoon, and I delivered the message during the morning session. The challenge came from our guest speaker for the afternoon chapel.

During the morning chapel, a homeless person came off MacDill Avenue. He was dressed in filthy clothes and was unshaven. He had a terrible body odor. I believe he was also wearing a hat and carried a bag with his belongings. My immediate consideration was the protection of the children under my leadership.

The children and the adults in attendance responded in various ways. When he sat in the pew, people moved over, not wanting to sit next to him. The boys and girls could not restrain themselves from looking back at the outsider. Needless to say, chapel ran over time. Imagine me running a little long!

The elementary school was having lunch. As we exited chapel and headed towards the fellowship hall, many of the elementary children began offering this fellow food and trying to welcome him. He walked out to the school courtyard and through the parking lot back onto MacDill Avenue. I did not know what was going on, and it was kind of scary.

Later that afternoon at the final chapel, this fine-looking gentleman entered as they were ready to introduce the speaker. He was neatly groomed, clean-shaven, and well-spoken. He began to teach from the book of Matthew.

"The King will reply, "Truly I tell you, whatever you did for one of the least of these brothers and sisters of mine, you did for me." (Matthew 25:40 NIV)

Without my knowing it, our youth pastor had arranged all of this. The homeless person from earlier was now our guest speaker, and he shared about how he was treated. Some were kind to him. Some offered him food. Some shunned him and moved away from him.

To this day, I have never forgotten that chapel. It was a powerful message and was right on target. It pierced my heart. As the speaker challenged the boys and girls with salvation, many of them came to the altar for first time commitments. Others came to reaffirm and to ask forgiveness. That day, the Holy Spirit visited us with power, might, and love.

Pedro and Maria

I first met Pedro and Maria at a Bayshore United Methodist Church service. As the service was about to close, the pastor asked if anyone needed prayer. A Cuban couple came to the altar, asking for healing prayer for Pedro's leg. Pedro had been a political prisoner in Cuba. As he attempted to escape, they shot him.

The bullet entered his hamstring and exited through his thigh. He suffered severe leg cramps and pain each day. The Lord led me to pray for him. I walked towards the altar and proceeded in anointing him with oil and asking God to heal him. Pedro also needed a job. I prayed for that, as I believe that God has anointed me to pray for people to obtain work.

One of our custodial staff unexpectedly resigned the very next day. I called Pedro and offered him the position. He accepted and was grateful and humbled.

As I got to know Pedro and Maria better, Pedro shared an incredible story of their escape from Cuba. A group of about 20 people planned to escape by boat. Pedro, who has many skills and talents, took a 15-foot wooden boat and extended it to 18 feet. He also made the sides of the boat higher. After many months of preparation, the group was ready to attempt their escape.

There were men, women, and children. A nurse, who planned to give them intravenous fluids to prevent dehydration, was among them. They had two outboard engines, one manufactured by Russia and the other by America.

The Russian motor was a diesel fuel operated engine. The American motor was gas operated. They only had one propeller. When they ran out of diesel fuel, they took the propeller off and threw the engine overboard. This made the boat lighter and sit up higher on the water. They had to wait several hours in order to get in the water to place the propeller onto the American made engine, as there were several sharks circling the boat.

They continued on their journey. Several days went by. There were heavy seas. People got sick. Others wanted to jump overboard and end their lives. Day after day, they were not sure of their survival. Pedro prayed to God that they would be safe in this ordeal.

Many Cubans make the 90-mile trek from Cuba to Key West and the lower part of Florida on the East Coast. Pedro's group chose to go another route, one that would lead them to Mexico. They hoped to navigate to the Grand Cayman Islands.

Late one night and in the midst of their depression, Pedro spotted some lights. They made it to the shoreline. They learned that it was not Grand Cayman but Cayman Brock. They were arrested and allowed to make a phone call to family or friends in the United States to have them wire money to get them out of jail. Once out of jail, someone gave them a GPS, and they plotted a course to Honduras.

There, they were arrested again and had to make more phone calls to the States. Once out of jail, they connected with a mule, someone who would guide them on their journey. The mule was on horseback. At some point, Pedro said that the man wanted one of the young girls and wanted her NOW.

The group told him he would have to kill them before they turned over any of their women. The mule never asked again for a woman. He led them across Honduras into Guatemala.

In the dark of the night, Pedro went in search of the Rio Grande River. To his surprise, it was not that far from where they were. Quietly, all 20 individuals moved towards the river while the mule slept. In some places, the Rio Grande River is shallow enough that one can walk or wade across. Other parts are too deep, and one must grab a log, board, or anything that floats. They were able to make it into Mexico. Upon arrival, they were arrested again. No doubt about it, it would take money to get out of jail in Mexico.

They made more phone calls to relatives and friends in the States. Once they obtained money, they paid another mule, who drove a van, to take them to the States illegally. For $300, the mule would take them as far as New Jersey. Arrangements were made. The money arrived. Everyone, except Pedro and Maria, were able to leave. Someone had stolen their money.

While in jail, Pedro and Maria survived by sewing and mending clothing for the prison guards. Pedro is also somewhat of an artist. He made cards that rivaled Hallmark. At one point, Pedro taught English in Cuba. He could also repair shoes and even make a pair of shoes. There was a period of time where Pedro fished commercially. Pedro truly was a "jack of all trades" and a survivor.

The couple finally rounded up enough money to get to New Jersey. They were homeless and living in a public park.

Somehow, they worked their way to Tampa. The Refugee Community Network found two men who would take them in. These two men worked at Bayshore.

The arrangement was that Maria would cook and clean. Once he was employed, Pedro would pay a fair price for the one room in which he and Maria lived. After several months, Pedro came to my office and told me he could not live with those two men any longer. They kept raising the rent and demanding more from Maria.

Pedro also shared that the individuals were heavy into pornography, and they were stealing from the school. The first thing I thought was to ask Pedro to invite me to the house. I took Betty and my camera with me. I saw a considerable number of removed items from our school. There were televisions, computer monitors, vacuum cleaners, gallons of floor wax, and many other janitorial supplies. They had established their own janitorial business on the side by using the school's supplies.

That afternoon, Pedro turned in his keys to the house. Pedro and Maria's belongings were in a black trash bag. I explained to Pedro that I was going to dismiss the two men the next day and offer Pedro and Maria those custodial positions. If they chose to accept, they could move into the school's maintenance house. While it was a mess, they could turn it into their home.

A friend put me in contact with a Tampa Police Department detective. Needless to say, the school got back everything that had been taken. Bayshore also put a stronger checks and balances in place to prevent further thefts.

Immediately, the teachers, parents, and school board members began to shower Pedro and Maria with a stove, a refrigerator, curtains, dishes, food, etc. Within a 30-day period, they had a nice place to call home. Now, the school had a live-in custodian. Pedro and Maria took personal ownership of the home and the school. Bayshore was their school!! While it lasted, the partnership was a great blessing to both this couple and the school. Today, Pedro and Maria live in Texas to be near one of Maria's daughters. They are doing well.

Coaching the Faith Warriors

1982-1983 Faith Warriors Basketball Team

At Bayshore, I had numerous occasions to do radical things. One of which was to schedule a basketball game between Bayshore and Lakeland Christian.

One of the assistant coaches at Lakeland Christian, Tim Strawbridge, was on the Lakeland High School team that Robinson High School beat in 1980 when I was the basketball coach. That was the game that ushered Robinson into the Final Four that year.

Tim went on to play basketball. I believe he played for the University of Florida and then transferred to the University of South Florida. I was told his dad purchased 100 tickets in advance for seating in the Lakeland Coliseum. That's how certain he was. That's how certain the Lakeland team was. They believed they would have a victory over Robinson High School and move on. That's not how it ended though. Robinson scored seven points in 17 seconds at the close of the game. One of those points was earned on a last-second shot. I'll never forget that game.

One of my other memorable games was the Bayshore – Lakeland Christian game. Lakeland Christian jumped out to a quick 16-point lead at the end of the first quarter. Tim Strawbridge was now one of the assistant coaches in that district game. Bayshore could not buy a basket if our lives depended on it.

One of my coaching techniques is to be able to control momentum or to take the momentum away from the opposition. At the start of the second quarter, Bayshore went into a full delay game, not intending to shoot for the entire quarter. The plan was to go in at half time and make some adjustments.

My point guard was right in front of our bench. I instructed him to stay right there and to not even dribble the ball. He was only to hold it. However, the rule back then was that the offense had to initiate play. You could do that by just crossing the timeline.

I instructed John Harvell to cross the timeline, stay there, and dribble the ball. Since they were up 16 points on the scoreboard, Lakeland decided that if we wanted to sit on the ball, they would let us do so.

John Harvell had a difficult time just standing there dribbling, knowing that his team was 16 points down.

I told John, "Wait until just inside 12 seconds, dribble to the wing where you like to shoot off the glass, and then bank it in."

Johnny did as he was instructed. He banked one off the glass. We were now down 14 points and momentum had been lost by Lakeland. I failed to mention the attitude of our fans at this point. They were questioning my decision to hold the ball when our team was down 16 points. They were aggressive, hostile, and certainly not very Christian-like. People at Bayshore had begun to take their basketball very seriously.

We came out in the second half and momentum shifted to Bayshore. In the closing moments two critical calls against Bayshore did not go our way. One was an offensive charging call and the other a traveling call on the fast break. We lost that game by 2 points.

Thinking Outside of the Box

On another occasion at another school in Lakeland, I needed a timeout that I didn't have. Once again, I cinched up my tie and walked out on the court towards the official. As he saw me coming, he started to back up.

He said, "You can't be out here."

I responded, "I know I can't."

As I continued walking towards him, he began to back up farther. I believe he thought I was going to physically accost him. Val Stevens, my assistant principal, and Mazie Young, my secretary, would always record the game off the radio. It was quite entertaining to listen to the recording later, on our way to another game.

"Mr. Valdes, the principal and coach, is aggressively going after the official."

Looking back on this, I can see that it did appear that I was going to do the official some harm. When he could not backup any farther, the official finally addressed the situation.

"I have to give you a technical."

I said, "That's all that I wanted from the beginning."

You see, I had used all my timeouts, and I needed to stop the game. I thought this was one way of doing so without being foul mouthed or verbally aggressive. In this case, I got the technical. I was able to make some adjustments and go on to win the game.

I am always thinking out of the box. I call timeouts under the basket, one pass from scoring. That's five timeouts per game and five opportunities to score. Every time the opponent loses possession, I believe it's a scoring opportunity for my team, and I have implemented scoring opportunities from every dead ball situation.

Herman and assistant coaches at BCS in 1991. L-R, Tom Dibble, Sam Lanier, Coach Valdes and John Harvill.

Scouting an opponent is extremely important in my opinion to be successful. One of my assistants or I have traveled all through the state of Florida to seek film on our opponents. At the conclusion of every basketball game, I went home to replay recordings of the tapes whenever they were available. This helped me to organize my practice session for the next day. Paying attention to details, even the most minute detail, can be the winning edge.

COURT *of* LEGENDS

FLORIDA ASSOCIATION OF BASKETBALL COACHES

2016

HERMAN VALDES
ROBINSON HS

- Compiled a 561-172 Record over 26 Years at Robinson HS & Bayshore Christian.
- 2 FHSAA State Runner-Up Finishes at Robinson in 1975 & 1980
- 2 FHSAA State Runner-Up Appearances with Bayshore Christian in 1987 & 1994
- Best Team: Robinson 1980
- Robinson Basketball Court Named After Him

Publix.

Induction into the Florida Association of Basketball Coaches , 2016

Philippines Missions Diaries

*T*HE FOLLOWING ARE EXCERPTS FROM *the diaries of our days on a mission to the Philippines. It is presented with minimal edits.*

While employed at Bayshore, it had been my desire to take three boys on a mission trip to the Philippines. I raised a considerable amount of money to be able to do that. Jonathan Johnson, Jonathan Fielder, and Anddrikk Frazier, "Smoking" Joe Frazier's nephew, were the boys chosen for the mission. Jonathan Johnson was 6' 6 or 7" at the time. Jonathan Fielder was 6' 4", and Anddrikk Frazier was 5' 10". My desire was for these three boys to experience sharing their faith in a second or third world country while having the Holy Spirit guide and direct them. I believed this experience would better able them to witness and be a positive influence on the rest of our student body once they returned home.

On April 28, 1993 and after several months of preparation and dealing with emotions and feelings, both mine
and Betty's, the hour of departure was at hand. Better, wonderful Betty, and I packed over 200 T-shirts and backpacks,
swim fins, and medicines for the boys and girls of South
Leyte, Philippines, and the surrounding islands attending a
youth conference where we were to minister. Basketball is
the number one sport in the Philippines. Every village and
every town had a basketball court. Every home had a hoop,
whether it was a pole with a hoop or a coconut tree with a
small hoop. They played with a small ball. Everyone wanted
to play basketball, so we took a lot of basketballs on that
trip. We had free-throw shooting contests and other drills to
give away basketballs as prizes. We donated several hundred
T-shirts we took on this trip.

On the morning of our departure, Betty fixed oatmeal for
breakfast. We quickly ate. I kissed Mel and hugged Sam, our
black Labrador retriever. The rest of the family said goodbye
earlier. We arrived at the airport at 6:35 a.m., five minutes
late. One of the boys arrived an hour late. We thought he
might not make the flight. The enemy certainly tried hard
to interfere with this mission. That's exactly why I believed
with all my heart that some wonderful things were going to
take place.

We flew from Tampa to Dallas, Texas. It was a great flight.
We had a light breakfast and flew to San Francisco. We saw
some great sites from the air: Salt Flats, Monument Valley,
and the snowcapped Rockies. In San Francisco, we changed
airlines to China Air. We took off at 3 p.m. PST/6 p.m. EST.
The China Air flight was first-class. The flight took 12 hours
and 45 minutes. That's a long time. We arrived in Taipei at
7:30 p.m. which was 7:30 a.m. EST. We flew the northern
route and saw the most awesome view of Alaska and its coast
that links to Russia.

We had to wait 30 minutes for the shuttle to the hotel.
We got to our rooms, ordered dinner, and paid a total of just

$45 USD for all five of us to eat. From this point on, it was no more water or ice without the pill to purify it. It was now Wednesday, April 29. We had been on the go for 30 hours.

The hotel rooms were small. Pastor Bruce Williams and I each had our own room. The boys had separate rooms with First John, Jonathan Johnson, and Second John, Jonathan Fielder, sharing a room. Anddrikk Frazier had his own room. After a good night's rest, the hotel gave us a wake-up call at 6 a.m. We had a breakfast buffet at the hotel which included eggs, rice, sausage, rice pudding, dried fruit, dried fish, and some other unidentifiable things.

At 8:40 a.m., we left for the airport and boarded China Air on our way to Manila, Philippines. On the flight to Manila, we had breakfast again – scrambled eggs mixed with squid. Great stuff!

On the airplane, I was informed that there was a 50% tax on every item that you brought into the Philippines. If an item is valued at $10, one would have to pay a $5 tax. I was sharing our mission with the lady sitting next to me on the flight to the Philippines. She said she worked for the airlines and would help. Going through customs was a piece of cake. God took care of that. The office was so engrossed with the size of the boys that they stared, asked questions about basketball, and wanted to know who the coach was. Then, they just waved us on.

As we approached the baggage counter to check in at immigration in the Philippines, we stood head and shoulders above everyone. We really stood out. In fact, some of the clerks were heard saying "NBA! NBA!" They thought our boys were professional basketball players.

We exchanged some money. The rate was $25.20 PHP to $1 USD. We then arranged for transportation at a cost of $5 USD per person. We, ourselves, loaded the 14 suitcases on the bus. Traffic was worse than anything any of us had ever seen. The horn rules in Manila. It took almost one hour to go three miles bumper-to-bumper. At the Cebu airport, we were charged $39 USD for being overweight with our luggage. It was a short one-hour flight to Cebu. The Gonzalez family was waiting with the "health wagon" that belonged to a friend. We had to shove ten people and all luggage in the wagon. When we arrived in Cebu, we had a snack of mangoes, rice, chicken, Coke, and mango preserves. We certainly had been eating a lot.

Around 5 p.m. that day, the boys spotted a basketball game being played on a hill. We set up shop on the basketball court where a water buffalo had been walking around and defecating wherever it pleased. The court itself was dirt, and the basket was mounted on a pole. When we dribbled the ball, we had to make certain the ball didn't go into a pile of dung. Once the boys started doing drills, a large crowd gathered to watch them dunk the ball. After we had their attention, we began to share the gospel of Jesus Christ.

We didn't go to bed until 11 p.m. that day. Pastor Bruce crashed at 8 p.m. He was exhausted. He's great to travel with. Bruce was a real buddy. I missed my family dearly, and I would have liked to share this experience with them. I hoped that we could all come back someday.

On May 1, we were awakened at 4:30 a.m. by roosters. Breakfast was at 6:30 a.m. We enjoyed mangoes, chicken, rice, eggs, bread, and coffee. We ate, and the family ate the leftovers. We made certain to leave enough. That afternoon, we did some shopping and experienced halo-halo, Filipino ice cream. This frozen dessert was made with shaved ice, evaporated milk, and various ingredients including ube (a type of sweet potato), sweetened beans, coconut strips, pineapple, corn, etc. It was very, very tasty.

Aly Gonzales, our host, turned 64 on May 3. My daughter, Debbie, has the same birthday. Aly's wife's birthday was on May 2. On May 1, we treated Aly and his family, approximately 14 people in all, to a very nice dinner at a local restaurant on a hill that overlooked a large portion of Cebu.

May 2 was another early day. We were up at 4:30 a.m. Would you believe that I was getting up at 4:30 a.m. for anything other than fishing? That morning, it sounded like an animal grand band outside our window. The roosters, maybe 20 of them, were crowing. Dogs were barking. Chickens were clucking. It really sounded like a symphony.

Again, breakfast consisted of coffee, mangoes, pineapple, chicken, and, of course, rice. Our 6 a.m. Bible devotions were great. Bruce led the three boys and me. After breakfast, we left to exchange money and to go shopping. We picked up some great buys. For lunch, we had pizza at Shakey's. For nine of us to eat and enjoy three pitchers of Coke, the cost was $18 USD.

At 5:30 p.m., we had to hire two cabs in addition to the pickup truck owned by Aly to get everyone and our luggage to the ferry. Aly had already left for South Leyte. The ferry was scheduled to leave at 8 p.m., so we needed to arrive at 7 p.m. It was dark and pretty intimidating. There were lots of hungry people asking for handouts or to carry our luggage. We decided to do it ourselves in shifts, as there were over 14 pieces of luggage. We had four inside cabins with air conditioning; however, the cabins were cramped and not very clean. The common restroom facilities were worse than awful. I took a picture of the facilities.

We finally got settled and went out on deck to dry, as we were soaked with perspiration. Around 9:30 p.m., an announcement was made for everyone to go to their sleep area and await inspection. They were looking for stowaways. We finally went to sleep around 3:30 a.m.

We arrived in South Leyte on May 3. That afternoon, we had a free-throw shooting contest and gave away two basketballs to the winners. There were two age groups: 12 and under and 13 and older. The whole town seemed to be there. Our boys conducted the contest and distributed candy to all the children in attendance. I instructed the Filipino boys in proper shooting mechanics. It was extremely hot that day.

It was now time to eat again. This time, it was pork chops, mangoes, pineapple, and rice. We started this day at 4:30 a.m., and it was now 6:30 p.m. We would not get to sleep until after 11 p.m. because it was just too hot. That evening, we left for Mindanao on the "Gospel Boat." This was an overnight crossing. From this point on, our facilities went downhill. I felt that we adjusted though and were ready for whatever was ahead. I had been feeling great, but this next week was tough.

We landed in Mindanao, and Philip Gonzalez, Aly Gonzalez's son, was there to greet us. What a pleasant surprise! We all crammed into a small pickup. There were 10 people and 14 pieces of luggage. It was also raining for the first time in over eight weeks. We stopped and had breakfast at a small restaurant in Butuan City. That was a nice way of breaking up the trip from the ferry to the church. It took over an hour to get to the church which was where we stayed for one week. Both room facilities assigned to us were sub, sub-par by our standards.

Later, we went to town to have lunch and do a little shopping. We were going from place to place on bicycle-driven cabs. We drew a crowd wherever we went. We took a great trip through the marketplace, and I took lots of photos to share with the people at home.

That night, Pastor Bruce and I shared a message at the church. The people were so happy that we had journeyed so far to be with them.

I really, really missed Betty. When I take these trips, I want her to always understand that a vital part of me is missing. I am not complete without her; however, I really needed to take this trip for me spiritually. Through this mission, I believed God would make me a better man to lead others to Him. I also missed Debbie, Kim and Mel, my daughters, very much. The Filipinos really expressed a desire to meet Mel, my youngest. There are so many things she would have loved to see in the Philippines; however, the facilities are rough due to a lack of cleanliness, clean showers, and clean toilets. I prayed that Debbie had had a safe and wonderful birthday. I missed everyone, but we were just getting started. There was much work yet to be done.

I spoke with Philip Gonzalez about a venture to buy prawns and ship them to our hometown of Tampa by air express. The wholesale market price in the Philippines was less than $3.50 per pound. The shrimp are huge, seven to eight inches long. I thought it could be a real moneymaker.

We were busy the next day with a courtesy visit to the mayor to gain his permission to use the town gym. The mayor suggested, however, that we postpone the meeting until 9 a.m. on May 5, so we could meet with all town officials.

We decided to make a trip to buy bicycles and rice and meat to feed the 150 to 200 kids attending the Youth Conference. Bruce and I jumped on the back of two motorcycles for a 40-mile one-way trip to Butuan City to purchase eight bicycles. We shopped around for the best price and finally settled on paying $1400 PHP or $56 USD for the bikes. We also bought bottled water and three mosquito nets for the boys. They had been attacked by bugs. Anddrikk Frazier's lips were very swollen, so we purchased an ointment to relieve the swelling.

We stopped by a two-acre rice field owned by Philip Gonzalez and visited with the squatters who cared for the property. There was a father, a mother, and five children living in a room that was the size of our kitchen back at home. It had an additional room upstairs. We learned they were new converts. We took some photos, prayed for them, and left them $100 PHP.

On our return from the city, Bruce led the kids at the conference in praise and worship.

One would have thought that our boys were NBA stars on tour. When they went to the common water trough to shower, more than 50 people came out to watch. The people were in awe of the height of the boys. Later, Bruce and I walked to the place where the boys had bathed. The water came from a cold spring and felt great on our bodies.

On the walk home, we visited a family mining gold in their backyard. They brought mud from the mountains, washed it, and panned it. The next day, we saw the final product of their mining.

Kids from all over the islands began to arrive to attend the Youth Conference. It was almost 3 p.m., and they would continue to arrive into the night. This particular week, the lights came on at 8 p.m. and went off at 4 a.m. This meant we got to sleep with a fan on. Praise the Lord!

We went into town to play a game of basketball. I even played, but I guarded a very short, older Filipino. It was so hot. When the game was over, we gave the ball away. I wanted to stop and invite everyone to church, but Philip said that would not be wise without the mayor's permission. From there, we went back to the well for another bath. I believe that was our third of the day. I was very tired, and I had developed a sore throat. I prayed and believed that the sore throat would heal. Praise GOD! It did!

I'm not sure about the scheduling of the basketball clinic. There appeared to be some confusion among the leaders of the town as to when to have it. In all fairness to them, they had planned on May 8 – 9, but that was when we had planned to take Pastor Bruce to South Leyte to visit all the little island churches.

He kept saying, "Herman, what have you gotten me into?"

The service that evening was wonderful. It began at 6:30 p.m. and finished near 10 p.m. Pastor Bruce did a great job preaching from Joshua 19:1 – 9. Later, an invitation was given to those serious about entering the ministry and those with physical problems. The kids in the service were not crying. They were weeping. There were such serious needs there, but no one complained. Several people were slain in the Spirit. I had not talked to the boys yet about what they witnessed.

I got to sleep around 2:30 a.m. I had already been up for 30 minutes, and it was now 7 a.m. Ouch! Not much sleep.

It was now May 5. During the night, I heard a gecko. This kind of lizard makes awful bloodcurdling sounds. I had not seen one yet. They told me it looks like a crocodile that is about 16 inches long.

They started breakfast. Every meal included rice. They added something called sticky rice. It looks like wild rice that has been mixed with brown sugar. Classic Coke is served with every meal including breakfast. I planned to cut back on the Coke that evening. It might have been the caffeine that caused me to have stomach problems and/or difficulty falling asleep.

Over the next three days, Pastor Bruce and I conducted three two-hour clinics on planning and goal setting. It was difficult to tell how successful they were, as we did not use an interpreter.

We made a courtesy call to the mayor and his staff. They gave us a wonderful welcome, and pictures were taken. The mayor wanted us to conduct an exhibition in the town gymnasium. We rode to the mayor's office on bicycles, and the mayor brought us back in a car. He also ordered a Filipino flag to be made for us to bring home. We presented him with a nice Bayshore Christian School pullover short-sleeved shirt and a BCS baseball cap, sealing our friendship.

Later, that day we went to the beach to cool off. It was beautiful. You could see a volcano on the horizon. The water was clear, and there were children everywhere. For some reason, everyone wanted their photograph taken and for us to carry them to America.

That same afternoon, I was upstairs, writing and resting. There was a noisy volleyball tournament taking place outside. The kids, 100 percent of them, were having a great time. I learned that many more kids had planned to come to the Youth Conference but did not because of a lack of finances.

That night, I was prepared to preach on my favorite Psalm, Psalm 34, but God had other plans. "Be Strong and Courageous" was the theme of the summer camp. This was taken from Joshua 1:9. It was a wonderful evening. Anddrikk Frazier gave his testimony. Afterwards, I could not preach, as the praise and worship was so intense. There was a call for salvation, a call to recommit, and a call for the infilling of the Holy Spirit. Each time, large numbers responded. Our three boys also responded to an altar call. We then called for those who were ill and those with parents or grandparents that were ill. Praise and worship continued the entire time. We began the service at 6 p.m. and finished at 10 p.m. There was no air-conditioning, and the pew seats were hard. Not a single person complained.

It was now May 6. I slept okay that night; however, people were up singing praises at 4:30 a.m., along with the constantly crowing roosters. We tried again to use the gym for instruction. By this time, my body was very tired, and I kept waking up with headaches. The journey was worth it. I enjoyed watching God work in the life of Anddrikk Frazier.

Each day, our laundry was done for us. There was a lot of it. It was so hot. The boys kept playing basketball and dirtying more clothes each game.

We finally got the okay to use the town gym for an exhibition game against the local boys. The heat did a number on Jonathan Fielder and Jonathan Johnson, but Anddrikk Frazier had too much heart to quit. The entire police force was there, along with approximately half the town. After the game, the Chief of Police wanted a basketball. I had him shoot free throws to earn it. There was also a young man. He had played against us and was a very good player. He very politely asked if we would give him one of our basketballs because they were so much better than what they had. It was an inexpensive $13 USD rubber ball from the States, but he was overjoyed to receive it.

After the game, one of the player's mothers wanted my Georgia Bulldog shirt. Maybe she was impressed with my playing ability? That's just a joke. This lady was the mother of Truman, a boy I had prophesied over the last time I visited. This was my second trip to the Philippines. Truman was now in his third year of high school and played the drums for his church.

For $0.40 USD, Pastor Bruce and I could ride in a rickshaw wherever we wanted to go. After the game, we decided to go back to the well to bathe and shave, as Pastor Bruce was preaching that night. The trip to and from the well was about 2 miles.

I know Betty was praying for me. I felt her prayers and her love. I missed air-conditioning, my king-size bed, and my pillows. I forgot to bring a small pillow with me on the trip. By this time, that was no longer important. The heat was even more bearable.

On the next day, May 7, I taught for two hours in the morning about using four personality types to form groups. I challenged the leadership with S.W.O.T. (Strengths, Weaknesses, Opportunities, and Threats), a program used for managing a school, church, business, etc.

That was a good day. All three boys had performed "Transformed", a rap. That was outstanding. The boys had been sharing their testimony, raising their hands in praise, and laying hands on others and praying for them. That day, our hosts roasted a pig and had a party for us.

That afternoon, we packed our belongings and chartered a Jeepney, which was much safer than public transportation, for $500 PHP to drive us to Surigao. I thought the Jeepney would accommodate five to eight people. Somehow, a total of 21 ended up on the bandwagon. It was so hot that I rode on the running board on the back of the Jeepney. I viewed the beautiful countryside as we traveled. It was a two-hour drive. We then boarded the ferry for a three-hour trip headed to Liloan, South Leyte. As we traveled, the facilities continued to decline. I hoped and prayed there would not be as many bugs at our next stop as there were at our last stop.

When we arrived, it was late and already dark. We spent that night with wonderful Martha and her husband, José, in a room that was normally a rental. We slept on grass mats and with no air conditioning. There were roaches and geckos everywhere in our bedroom. It was located upstairs above a bakery that was operated during daylight hours. Pastor Bruce and I managed to joke and laugh about the circumstances and the adventure God had set before us. Bruce was so much fun to travel with.

A rooster started crowing at 1 a.m., then at 2 a.m., and then at 3 a.m. We got fed up and started to throw hard candy at it. As mentioned, we were sleeping upstairs. Needless to say, we missed the rooster. I gave up, put on a headset, and turned up the volume. It really worked, as I was finally able to get some sleep. The next morning, we found hard candy everywhere on the ground.

That day, we waited on the high tide to take an outrigger canoe to visit the island churches. Again, there were hundreds of people watching us and our baggage. We could have managed with half the clothing we brought, as everyone we visited and stayed with did our laundry. We were treated wonderfully well. It was now off to breakfast.

High tide was at 11:30 a.m. The boys were playing basketball at 6:30 a.m. The gym was again filled with people watching. After the game, we walked over to a little waterfront café and had a Coke. We then loaded the canoe with what was left of the T-shirts to be distributed to children who did not have the opportunity to attend the Youth Conference. We traveled by canoe for about 15 miles to reach the first church.

The church was small but was exceptionally clean. It was on the island of Malang. The pastor at this little church was a woman. She had a one-week-old baby. We gave her $250 PHP. She was so thankful that she began to weep. We prayed with the people there, and Bruce gave away more money. Then, it was on to the next church.

I was taking pictures in the area when I spotted a tough looking and weather-beaten Filipino with a homemade speargun and homemade swim goggles. He also had a home-made swim fin. Yes, it was only one. It was circular shaped like a plate. It was big enough for two binders to slip his feet into. He swam like a dolphin with the motion of both legs together and working at the same time. I made friends with him and gave him a pair of swim fins we had brought from the States. I borrowed his homemade swim goggles. He made them with the shell of a coconut and Coke bottle glass. They worked surprisingly well, and I looked around the reef with them. It was beautiful scenery.

Homemade Swim Goggles

The old spear fisherman had trouble using the fins that I had given him. The pastor's husband really wanted them, so I bought the fins back for $10 PHP and gave them to the pastor's husband. Everyone was happy. I did see the spear fisherman swim down approximately 30 feet and spear several really small fish. The spear was thinner than a pencil. I guessed that would be his dinner that night.

We returned late, took a shower, and had dinner. The menu was grilled fish, rice, mangoes, pineapple juice, and orange juice made from Tang. I found it difficult to sleep. I tossed and turned most of the night. At 1:30 a.m., a rooster started crowing. Bruce threw a belt buckle and hit it. Feathers flew everywhere, and the rooster took off, at least for a while.

Around 4 a.m., we heard this terrible squealing sound. The pig, the same one I had taken a picture of the night before, was being butchered in preparation for a picnic later that day. They prepared the pork by seasoning the individual ribs with salad oil, pepper, and ginger. Then, they rolled it in flour and fried it. Some of the pork was also seasoned with salt, pepper, and ginger mixed with Sprite. It marinated for several hours and was grilled. It was all very tasty. There were over 60 people at the picnic. It took two round-trip boat rides to transport everyone.

Before the picnic, we traveled by outrigger canoe to a beach house that looked like it might have belonged on an island paradise. The owner of the house was a poet. She was well-respected and very well-known in the Philippines for her poetry. Bruce and I climbed to the top of a mountain near the house and took some great photos. Later, we swam and collected some shells which I later boiled to remove the animal. On return to the house, I waited for Bruce to finish bathing. It seemed as though he took forever.

On May 10, we left for Leyte on the Gospel Boat, an outrigger canoe, for a three-hour ride. We then took a six-hour ferryboat ride back to Cebu. We traveled to Maasin City to board the ferry. The city's name means salty. We arrived at about 3 p.m. We could not find dock space, so we beached the canoe and formed a line to unload it. I originally thought that there would only be seven of us on the canoe, but we actually had a boatload of 22 people, mostly teenagers. The ferry to Cebu did not depart until 10 p.m. The ferry was already at the dock, but it was not going anywhere any time soon, as the captain had gone to his home island to cast his ballot because it was election day.

We were there with our 14 pieces of luggage, waiting to board a ferry that would not leave until 1 a.m. now. What were we to do in a rough looking port for eight hours? There was a holding area for passengers, but it strongly smelled of urine. I would not have put my dog, Sam, in there. I suggested that we find a hotel.

We booked three rooms at $30 PHP per person. That was a dollar and change in USD. This was not a very desirable hotel. Only one of the rooms had a toilet and a faucet to wash up. We walked around town, and I made a phone call home. We ate some ice cream. It was a real treat! I think I ate a whole pint. We then went back to the hotel to wait. The room was so hot that we decided to have a picnic-style dinner in the lobby. After, we sat on the veranda to observe the people below.

I was watching a man. He appeared to be intoxicated. He was only wearing a swimsuit and was making a doll house out of a cardboard box. He was sitting on a table, singing, and acting weird. Soon, a young boy, maybe 16, joined him on the table that was about the size of a ping pong table. The two joked around for a while, and the young boy fell asleep. Two older boys, also teenagers, came and attempted to take the man's cardboard doll house. The young boy awakened and began arguing with them.

As Bruce and I watched, one of the boys, who was wearing black and white shorts, stabbed the young boy protecting the man's belongings. The young boy began to stagger. I wanted to help him, but I was apprehensive and did not know if I should get involved.

It was evident that the boy was severely injured. I took my money belt off and consulted Bruce and Aly Gonzales as to whether we should attempt to assist the young boy. Bruce and I decided to go down on the street to help. We talked to the boy and discovered he had about a four-inch and fairly deep stab wound. It didn't appear to be life-threatening. The police came, and we gave a description of the individuals involved. The police said they knew the offenders, so we left the scene to return to the hotel, as we did not want to be delayed or called as witnesses to give our testimony to this occurrence.

We quickly packed our belongings and made a beeline for the ferry. By then, things had cooled off quite a bit. I sat on top of a double bunk. The ferry was open air. It was quite nice. There was a half moon. The stars were out, and we finally left at 1:30 a.m. We were scheduled to arrive in Cebu by 8 a.m.

At 6:05 a.m., I heard a rooster crow. I just knew there was one on this ferry, but no one else heard it. There were not many passengers on this trip, and the restrooms were clean! Praise the Lord! God must have poured out an extra blessing on us that day. The whole cruise deck was open air. I slept well, really well. It was not as long as I would have liked, but it felt really good to sleep.

I had eight shots left on a roll of film, so I decided to take some pictures as we approached Cebu. We were maybe 40 minutes from docking. I could see the city. It was crowded as we got off the dock. Many Muslims were there and were begging just like last time. We tossed coins wrapped in pesos in order to give the paper pesos some weight. They were thrilled to receive the money.

It was good to see one of the young men, who worked with Aly Gonzales, with the truck to take us to the pastor's house in Cebu. There, we ate breakfast, kicked back, and took a shower. I started feeling tired. I thought my sugar level was possibly off a bit. I took two aspirin and a water pill to start the process for boarding the plane for a long flight home. We got up at 5:30 a.m. for breakfast. At 6 a.m., we went to the currency exchange to get enough pesos for the shuttle to the Manila International Airport. Per person, it was $5 USD or $650 PHP plus tips.

Our flights had been confirmed. While waiting to board the plane, we went shopping at White Gold. I bought some silk scarves. We left Cebu for Manila around 11 a.m., departed Manila for Hong Kong at 2:20 p.m., and arrived in Hong Kong at 4:40 pm.

On arrival in Hong Kong on May 12, a limousine took us to the Omni Hotel. I could hardly wait to get home. Only the power of the Holy Spirit could have taken me from my home, my family, my friends, and everything I love doing to make a trip such as this. I knew this mission was Holy Spirit directed and led.

When we arrived at the Omni Hotel, we had a moment of concern. Somehow, the accommodation arrangements for the three boys had not been made. Like usual, God took care of it, and we were given two beautiful suites.

The first thing Bruce did was take a bubble bath and a shower. The man must have been in there for an hour. It was actually only 30 minutes. Then, it was my turn.

We hit the streets around 8 p.m. and ate at a Pizza Hut. The pizza was terrible. We caught a cab to Temple Street. This street looks like a large flea-market. I purchased a few things. I got a Nintendo Game Boy for my grandson, Matthew, and two silk ties. I also bought a beautiful silk scarf with earrings to match for my wife. We walked around until after 11 p.m. We were dead tired by that time. I continued to think about how wonderful it would be to have my wife here with me. I made a note that we must come before 1997, as this was when the country would transition from British rule to Communist China rule.

At the hotel the next morning, we had an American breakfast of apple juice, pineapple slices, croissants, pancakes, and cereal. If you ordered it on Friday, it included sausage and coffee and only cost $14 USD. Hong Kong is a shopper's paradise. I bought the Sharp model organizer for $62, half as much as it would cost in the States.

It was time to take the boys home. They tried to make friends and act like adults, but they were now acting more and more like the teenagers they were. We drove to the China airport in a Mercedes-Benz that was worth $81,000 USD at the time. The plane left for Taipei at 12:50 p.m. We had a two-hour layover. I hoped we would get good seats.

The seats were okay. The flight was only an hour and 20 minutes. We ate rice and prawns, salad, and dessert, and we drank coffee. It was incredibly good. We then sat at gate five waiting to board the long flight to Los Angeles. We had an hour delay taking off for Los Angeles because a movie screen was broken. What a waste of valuable time.

We flew to Los Angeles at an altitude of 38,000 feet. We were served a meal consisting of meat, vegetables, bread, coffee, and Coke. It was not bad. What was bad was trying to get comfortable after tossing and turning for several hours. I did sleep some.

When I woke up, they were serving breakfast. The choice was asparagus or something else. I remember thinking the latter was the best of both choices. Boy, I was wrong. I got a rush of nausea. I got clammy. I was sick to my stomach. It did not pass until I upchucked.

We missed our connecting flight from Los Angeles to Tampa. Instead of arriving in Tampa at 1 a.m., we would arrive at 8:10 a.m. if all went as scheduled. We were all lying around at the airport in Los Angeles. I did go straight to the floor to get rid of the dizziness I was experiencing. At 7:33 a.m., we got something to eat. I had to take it easy on my stomach, as I didn't want to get sick on the plane on the way to Tampa. After the delay, everything went as planned, and we arrived safely in Tampa to a crowd of waiting family and friends whose prayers got us through.

The Gospel Boat

Let me tell you a short story of the "Gospel Boat" and how it got started. Aly Gonzalez had gone to the fish market to purchase fish. The fish was wrapped in an edition of the *Tampa Tribune*, Tampa's local newspaper. In the paper, there was an article about an attorney. He was helping a minister with the purchase of a boat to be used for ministry. That attorney was Dallas Albritton.

Aly Gonzales wrote to the *Tampa Tribune* and obtained the address for Dallas Albritton. Dallas responded to Aly and raised funds to provide an outrigger canoe. This was the Gospel Boat we rode on. It was approximately 30 feet long. From outrigger to outrigger, it was maybe 20 feet wide.

Prior to my third trip to the Philippines, I visited with Dallas Albritton. Knowing I had a visit planned to the city of Cabadbaran in the Philippines, Dallas wanted me to purchase 10 computers and other electronics to be delivered to a school that was operated by the Gonzalez family. He also gave me a $100 bill to be presented in thankfulness to a lady he had met on a prior visit. She provided him with some medical attention and a pair of shoes to relieve his badly aching feet.

Dallas Albritton, a highly respected attorney and spirit-filled Christian, helped develop the Agape Evangelistic Mission, the organization from which I obtained my ordination on April 20, 2008.

Dallas said, "Herman, I want you to find a woman, Alicia, in Cabadbaran and give her this $100 bill. Remind her of when she assisted me with shoes on a prior visit."

I responded, "Dallas, you want me to travel 12,500 miles to the island of Mindanao, locate this woman whose surname you do not know, and give her $100?"

"That's exactly what I want you to do, Herman."

On this trip, I was determined to take Betty with me, as I was going to perform a Filipino wedding. Let me share with you about a God-ordained meeting of two people. A good friend of ours, Jerri Pippin, was working at Kindred Hospital in Tampa. There, she met a young nurse, Zilpha. Jerri shared with Betty and me that this young woman was all by herself and away from her home in the Philippines. It was her birthday. In celebration of her birthday, Zilpha took a photo of herself holding a cupcake with a candle and sent it to her parents in the Philippines. Jeri knew I had been to the Philippines. She thought we could perhaps minister to Zilpha, so she would feel welcome here.

When I shared this with Betty and her sister, Louise, we decided to meet this young woman and take her to dinner to celebrate her birthday. We went to Olive Garden in St. Petersburg. Sitting around the table, I began to ask Zilpha to tell us about herself. Zilpha said that she was from the island of Mindanao. I told her I had been there. I asked what town she was from. Sure enough, I'd been there also. I shared with Zilpha that I had been in the Philippines for a Youth Conference that was facilitated by Aly Gonzalez and his son, Philip.

Zilpha said, "I was at that Youth Conference. My father, Sam Salar, studied under Aly Gonzalez. My father is also a minister in Cabadbaran."

I invited Zilpha to church and to Sunday school. I proceeded to share with Scott Burkett that we were going to have a guest in Sunday school. Scott had been single for quite a few years and was very anxious to meet this young Filipino nurse. Not long after that, Scott and Zilpha began dating. A little over a year later, they planned a wedding and asked if I would consider performing the ceremony. I told them that I would be honored. That was a long way to go just for a wedding, so we decided to combine the wedding with a mission trip. We wanted to spiritually minister and to be able to feed and provide other amenities to the people in the Philippines. Through friends and church members, we raised nearly $10,000 to be spent on ministry there. We each paid for our own flights, accommodations, etc. We planned to stay 21 days.

Scott, Betty, and I stayed in a compound with adequate security. We had a comfortable bed and hot running water. Each morning, we gathered for breakfast at the compound. Then, we were picked up by Jeepney or by a motorcycle to be transported into town to minister to the people. That was an incredible mission trip led by the Holy Spirit.

Traveling to the Philippines is not an easy journey. It requires numerous hours on an aircraft. Meanwhile, I was a little intimidated by the 28-page notebook that Zilpha handed to me explaining the whole Filipino wedding ceremony. God is so good though. While we were in the Philippines just prior to the wedding, we visited a small Bible college that was sponsored by Philip Gonzalez. Students were practicing performing a wedding. These were young pastors in training, and they were doing a hands-on mock wedding in preparation for their graduation requirements. I was able to observe all the different ceremonies of a Filipino wedding.

After the mock wedding, we went to a beach. I thought it was for a picnic. However, it was a hands-on practice session for the students. This time, it was for a funeral. The bridegroom from the mock wedding was now posed as the corpse for the funeral with Kleenex stuffed in his nose and his ears. He was dressed to the hilt in his wedding attire with a native shirt.

I looked at Betty and asked, "They're not really going to do this, bury him. Are they?"

Sure enough, they dug a hole, placed the young man in, and proceeded to cover him right up to his chin. When the funeral was over, it was time to walk into the water and watch as the students administered a mock baptism.

We visited with Zilpha's mom and dad and their church. They displayed a large banner, welcoming Herman, Betty, Scott, and Zilpha. Shortly after our arrival at Sam's, Zilpha's dad's home, I asked if he knew of a lady by the name of Alicia.

Much to my surprise, his response was, "Yes, she's a church member. She will be here this evening."

Only God can do this! We were 12,500 miles away, and there was Alicia! I told her the story of Dallas and the shoes. I took a picture with her. I later delivered it to Dallas back in Tampa. She recalled the incident of the shoes and was incredibly grateful to Dallas for the money.

While in Cabadbaran, we shopped for dried fish, canned goods, and hundreds of pounds of rice. These items were put into food baskets to be distributed to those in need. We went from village to village and home to home distributing the food and praying for the people. While there, we also arranged for water pipes and plumbing to be installed in Pastor Salars' home, so they would have running water.

At Phillip Gonzalez's church, we presented the computers that Dallas Albritton had bought for the school Phillip's church sponsored. We also preached at the church and prayed for the people in healing lines for hours.

After completing our ministry to the people in Cabadbaran, it was time for the wedding in Butuan. Scott looked grand in his tuxedo, and Zilpha was beautiful. She looked like she had just walked out of a storybook. The ceremony included several rituals: The Ceremony of the Cords, The Ceremony of the Coins, and The Ceremony of the Bible. Ten or 12 couples spoke into the lives of the couple. It was a beautiful wedding and a spectacular reception.

After arriving back in the States, Scott and Zilpha wanted to have another ceremony, so Scott's family and friends could attend. A second ceremony was held at Bayshore United Methodist.

Returning to Monroe

Monroe
Middle
School

A T SOME POINT, I KNEW that I was going to need
to return to Hillsborough County Public Schools. This
was necessary in order to complete my retirement requirements. It would also allow me to take advantage of the ben-
efits of cashing out my sick days, vacation days, etc.

I was working out at a local spa. Bill Pent, a friend of mine
and the principal of Monroe Middle School, asked me what
my plans were for the future. I told him that I planned to
apply to the school system for several different positions to
complete my retirement plans.

Bill shared with me that one of his assistant principals
was planning to retire. The school's reputation, climate, and
culture needed a shot in the arm. He thought that my professional background and my location a mile from Monroe
made me a strong candidate for the position. He asked if I
was interested.

I had to go through all the procedures and interviews. There were several strong candidates interviewing for this position. I attended a board meeting and was officially approved to be the assistant principal. Five years later, I went through the same process to become the principal.

As if it were yesterday, I remember my first day on the job as assistant principal. As I was walking the halls, three good-sized young men, locked arm-in-arm, came running through the hallways, knocking down any boy or girl who was in the way. My first official act was to suspend these young men, as they were being bullies and endangering the health and well-being of our students.

As assistant principal for student affairs, I was responsible for discipline, extracurricular activities, and anything else that the principal felt I needed to do or be involved with. The faculty was so gracious to share with me that they had been praying for a Christian administrator. They were literally excited for this answered prayer.

Those five years were preparing me for the larger task at hand. I was going to become principal.

One day, I needed a ride to school, as my vehicle was being serviced.

I called my boss and said, "Bill, can you swing by and pick me up on the way to work?"

"Of course," he said.

When he picked me up, he was dressed in shorts and a T-shirt. That was not his style.

I inquired, "What's up with your dress?"

He said, "This is my last day."

He drove a Bronco. In the back, there were several empty boxes. He carried them to his office to empty his personal belongings from his desk drawers and file cabinets. He put his school keys on the desk and said goodbye. That's how Bill Pent walked away from the school. For approximately six weeks, Monroe didn't have a principal. Instead, we had two assistant principals acting in that capacity.

The assistant principal for curriculum was a strong person. She was very opinionated and a good disciplinarian. I remember telling her that I was applying for the principal position. She responded that she was also applying for that same position. I told her that if she got the position that I could work for her. She told me that if I got the position that she could not work for me. I guess I shelved that comment to the back of my mind.

I was appointed principal. On my first day on the job, the assistant principal did not show up to school. Our area director, Ms. Robinson, was there bright and early in the morning to officially introduce me to the faculty as their principal.

My first day started without my assistant principal. During that same day, I received a phone call that my mother was gravely ill. I needed to leave. I quickly called Ms. Robinson to explain my dilemma and inform her that I was leaving the school in the hands of Joe Brown, the guidance counselor.

Once everything with my mother was stabilized, I returned to the school later that day. Several days went by. The assistant principal eventually came back to work. I grabbed a change of placement form, walked into her office, and closed the door.

I said, "You said that you could not work for me, so I have brought a change of placement form for you to fill out."

She quickly responded that she could separate her professional duties from her personal feelings and that she was willing to stay. She stayed until her retirement.

Important Research

I remember going to a middle school workshop where there was a lot of discussion about student-on-student aggression. Basically, the discussion was about bullying. In addition, there was discussion about keeping the school safe, as this was during the time of the Columbine shootings.

After the conference, I remember talking to Chuck Jaksec, our school psychologist, about the workshop. I told him that there had been multiple studies conducted regarding student-on-student aggression, student-on-teacher aggression, and teacher-on-student aggression. I wondered if anyone had studied parent-on-administration aggression.

Chuck's eyes lit up, as if someone had just planted a great idea in his mind. It was like a lightbulb had gone off, and Chuck began to do research. He received a small grant from Hillsborough County Public Schools to conduct a local survey. As the data was coming in, he realized that this needed to be broader. So, he sought a larger grant and received it as well.

You will not believe what he found out. He learned that administrators were so stressed that the heart attack rate among them had risen and illnesses were being attributed to stress. Literally, administrators had been verbally and physically accosted by angry parents and relatives.

About the same time, I had an incident in which I will try to capture for you. There were two boys in a physical education class. One boy, who had athletic ability, was continuously getting upset with the other boy, who had little to no athletic ability. It got to the point where the one boy was being verbally and physically bullied.

I had this brilliant idea. At the time, I thought it was brilliant. I scheduled a conference with the two boys and their parents. I also had my new assistant principal for administration, Joe Brown, attend the meeting.

I laid out the groundwork with a brief summary of the events that had taken place and were documented by the physical education teachers. At some point in the conference, the mother of one child began to make this a racial issue.

She pointed her finger at me and said, "If it was the other way around, we wouldn't be having this meeting. Would we?"

I basically said, "Ma'am, please don't point your finger at me and don't use that tone of voice."

She replied, "I'll point my damn finger at you if I want."

I concluded, "You are right. You can point your finger at whoever you chose, but you're not going to do it here. This meeting is over. I will let you know my response as to how I'm going to resolve this."

As I walked into the office the next morning, there was an individual with the physique of a weightlifter waiting to see me. Beth Larcom, my secretary, had forewarned me of this man wanting to meet with me first thing in the morning. So, I invited him into my office.

I sat behind my desk and asked him, "How may I help you?"

He began to lean forward in his chair and rested his arms on my desk in a position that I interpreted to be intimidating and aggressive. He began to point his finger at me. I do not know what it is about a finger being pointed at me, but I just don't like it. It was almost as if there was a script from the day before being played out.

I said, "Sir, let us not go there. Let us not be pointing fingers."

He responded, "I will do whatever I damn well please with my finger".

I responded, "You know. You're right. You could do whatever you want to do with your finger, but you are not going to do it here. This meeting is over."

He stood up and blocked the doorway. As I squeezed my way out of the door, he made a point to bump me. I eventually had to get the school resource officer involved. That was a stressful situation. I really thought that I might get hurt.

Here is another incident I had. Due to the angle of our parking spots at the front of the school, some parents parked diagonally, as they should. Others parked in the u-drive directly behind them and virtually blocked those who wanted to back out of the diagonal spot. Most often, people worked well together, and they allowed each other to back out and go forward. One day, a mother came looking for the resource officer. It just so happened that he was off campus that day.

I asked, "How may I help you?"

Shaken, she said, "There's someone parked behind me, and they won't let me out."

"I'll help you take care of this."

I walked towards the car. It was a yellow low-profile automobile. I think it was a Mustang. As the driver of the car saw me approaching, he cranked up his radio as loud as it would go. When I arrived, I had to lean over, and I put my hands on the roof of his car.

He responded, "Get your f—-ing hands off my car."

He began to open the door and step out. He appeared to be 6' 2 or 3". He had on work shorts, work boots, and a tight T-shirt. In athletic terms, this guy was ripped. I thought that I might get hurt. I had already decided that I was awfully close to kicking him in the place where most men don't want to get kicked. Then, I would just start running.

About that time, he saw the young girl he was there to pick up. He hollered as loud as he could to get her attention. Meanwhile, the rest of the parents were out of their cars and told me that he did that every single day. They had been putting up with his nonsense for a while.

The young girl got in the car, and he sped off in a dangerous manner. Remember that this was a school parking lot. There was no question that I was stressed out and frightened that I might get hurt. As I returned to the office, I asked Mrs. Larcom if she knew the name of the girl who was picked up. She answered to the affirmative. I gave her a short version of what I had just been through, and I asked her to get me the girl's mother's phone number. I proceeded to call her and requested she come to the school immediately, as I needed to speak with her privately. She was there within 15 to 30 minutes.

I asked her who the man was. She said it was her boyfriend. She allowed him to live with her in order to share expenses. I asked her if he had ever been abusive to her. She said that he had pushed her down several times. I told her that we were going to serve him with a trespass warrant. He was no longer allowed to drive on campus to pick up her daughter or to do anything at the school. If he insisted on coming on campus, he would be arrested.

I shared this with Chuck. Once again, his wheels just started turning. The following year, he and I attended a middle school conference where we presented a workshop on a topic that we thought would be interesting. We advertised it as "Parental Aggression on School Administrators." The room was filled to standing room only. Chuck continued to press forward with nationwide surveys on this topic. He wrote a book and gave me credit for my story of how I thought I was going to get my butt kicked, as this prompted him to do research on this topic. We discovered that this was a major problem among school administrators across the nation.

Discipline

I also remember another incident with another young boy. He was in my office again for poor behavior. We had previously gone through all the interventions: detention, in-house suspension, parent conferences, and work details. I had exhausted most of my options. We even sent home a change of placement letter to his mother, stating that if her son's behavior did not improve drastically that we would do a change of placement to an alternative school.

As I explained this to the mother, I gave her one more option. He was a very bright boy. Out-of-school suspension would have affected his grades. So, I suggested that I paddle him three times and send him back to class. She thought that was a good idea and agreed that I should do it. Corporal punishment was and still might be on the books in Florida, meaning it is legal or was legal at the time.

Convincing the young man that he needed to take his three whacks was a different matter. I believe I chased him around the desk several times. He finally accepted his punishment and stayed in school. That evening, Ms. Robinson, the Area Supervisor, was at the Interbay Little League Baseball Complex watching her nephew play baseball. The mother of the young man that I had paddled sat next to her. She proceeded to tell Ms. Robinson about the physical abuse that her child had to endure. The next morning, Ms. Robinson called Joe Brown. Normally, he would have handled the disciplinary action.

Ms. Robinson said to him, "You cannot and may not spank these children."

Joe responded, "It wasn't me, Ms. Robinson. It was Mr. Valdes."

Joe Brown had just thrown his boss under the bus, but I am not one to hold a grudge. When I was ready to leave Monroe, I gave Mr. Brown a strong recommendation, and he became the next principal.

Animals on Campus

While I was the assistant principal at Monroe, we had a faculty meeting to discuss bringing pets to school. Specifically, teachers bringing pets to school. There was an incident in Hillsborough County. A pony was brought in, and some children were injured. The County came up with a policy against teachers bringing pets in for show and tell. However, one of our teacher aides, who worked with children with special needs, decided to bring a beautiful, black Labrador dog to show to the kids.

At the time, our children with special needs were housed in portables at the front of the school. As the teacher led the dog up some steps to enter the portable, a large pit bull came out from under the portable and attacked the Labrador retriever. Children were screaming. The dogs were in a full survival and fighting mode in the classroom. The teacher quickly escorted the students out the back door. The administration was notified immediately. The resource officer, the assistant principal, the principal, and one of our coaches entered the portable and attempted to separate the dogs.

The pit bull refused to let go of the Labrador retriever's hind leg. Our coach grabbed a portable chair and pinned it on the pit bull's neck with a large amount of force. Still, the pit bull would not release the Labrador's leg. The office called animal control. In the portable, there were feces, vomit, and saliva flying all over the room. Finally, someone smothered the pit bull, so that it could not breathe. Then and only then, did the pit bull release its hold on the Labrador. We managed to drag the Labrador out and lock the pit bull in.

Animal control showed up. With a long snare, they lassoed the animal and dragged it to a secure screened cage. The animal reminded us of the movie, *Cujo*, which was about a demonic dog. As I walked in front of the dog and looked at him, his stare and his demeanor were unnerving.

I had to call the County office to report the incident. Parents had to be notified, and a crisis intervention team was summoned to minister to any traumatized children.

After numerous surgeries, the Labrador survived. The owner of the pit bull claimed that the dog had escaped his yard and obviously taken up residence under the portable. I am not certain whether the owner of the dog had to pay a penalty or a fine. This incident, however, further reinforced the new policy of not bringing animals to school for show and tell.

ROTC

A middle school ROTC program was something that no one in Hillsborough County had explored. After some research, we found that there was only one other middle school in the United States that had an ROTC program at that time. We had a young man, Mick Boddie, on our faculty. He was retired military and was very well-liked by students. His wife, Cindy, was our data processor. We discussed the possibility of an ROTC program with him and later with our faculty. Everyone was in favor of it.

Due to our close proximity to MacDill Air Force Base, an ROTC program seemed like the natural thing to have at Monroe. We chose the Army as the branch for our ROTC. I appointed Mr. Boddie to head up the program. He solicited help, and he had male and female full and casual uniforms donated. We were able to make ROTC a class at Monroe.

During the class, students performed drills, learned marching skills, discussed discipline, and received tips on how to make our school better and increase their rank just as in the military. This class helped greatly with boys and girls who were on the verge of disciplinary action. Wearing the uniform became a point of honor and was envied by many students. We implemented a color guard within the ROTC. During school functions, ROTC students served as ushers and escorted people to various school events.

❃ ❃ ❃

We organized a middle school trip to Washington, D.C. There, some of our ROTC members were to partner with the Marine Corps in the changing of the wreath at the Tomb of the Unknown Soldier. This was the highlight of the trip for our ROTC members.

We did not take every ROTC class member. We only took a select few. Altogether, there were approximately 50 of us on that trip – my wife and I, four or five other teachers as chaperones, and students. Late in the evening, we boarded a bus at Monroe. This allowed the boys and girls to get some sleep on the way to D.C.

After about a 10-hour drive, we were to meet up with another bus driver, who was scheduled to take over and finish the trip. Drivers were not supposed to drive for more than 10 hours straight. The relief driver did not show, so the current driver decided he would continue driving. My wife and I sat up front right behind the driver. We noticed that the bus driver was beginning to nod off, and the bus started to weave. I engaged the driver in conversation in the hopes of keeping him awake. It got so bad that I insisted he get off the interstate at the very next exit.

That exit did not have a reentry, so we drove about two to three miles on a very dark road. We finally came to a small church with a dimly lit parking lot. We drove into the parking lot and made several three-point turns with this massive bus. I had to step off the bus and guide the driver through this procedure. Once back on the road, the driver had to find a place to reenter the interstate. By this time, the driver was wide awake, and we successfully completed the trip.

The laying of the wreath at the Tomb of the Unknown Soldier was a major success. I am sure those students will remember that for the rest of their lives. We did the usual D.C. tourist excursions. Our visit to the Holocaust Museum was a very sobering experience.

I wanted things to happen on this trip that I had not planned for, but I was going to end up regretting it. My philosophy is that if we are in the business of education, we are in the business of educating all students, including those with learning disabilities, emotional disabilities, etc. Many of those children are on special medication. I failed, however, to take the special education teacher with me as a chaperone. The dispensing of the medication to these children was an involved procedure; however, we managed to do it and do it right.

We toured the Holocaust Museum. I gave all students instructions on how they were to behave. I felt comfortable that these were good kids. At the end of the tour of the Holocaust Museum, there is a shrine, a holy place with a menorah, candles, and photographs. This is a sacred place. I finished my tour quickly, so I could catch the students as they were finishing. I noticed three of our students with special needs were standing at the altar, and they were trying to blow out the candles. Yes, that is correct. They were trying to blow out the candles. I went berserk. I chewed on them from top to bottom and bottom to top.

"From this moment on, you're to go where I go and nowhere else. If I don't go, you don't go."

We visited the Museum of Natural History next. My new three best friends were with me. I needed to place a call to the school. I instructed my three best friends to walk around the elephant exhibit and read every plaque that had something to say about the elephant. With this, I stepped aside to place the call.

Another one of our teachers saw that the boys were not with me but were quickly walking round and round the elephant. If you've been to D.C. to this particular museum, you know that they have a large life-size mounted elephant on display. So, the teacher began to scold the boys.

With tears in their eyes, they said to her, "Mr. Valdes said to walk around the elephant."

That's not exactly what I said.

I actually said, "Read all there is to read about the elephant as you walk around it."

They were practically running around it.

That trip was so challenging that we only made it once more. If I ever do anything like that again, I will take our special education teacher and someone to dispense medication, not just for the needy students but for the principal.

Vacation Fiascoes

ONE SPRING BREAK, I DECIDED and convinced Betty
that we should go camping at Knights Key located in
Marathon, Florida. The Knights Key Campground is the last
land body before you drive over the Seven Mile Bridge. So, I
got the boat, boat trailer, and camping gear (tents, sleeping
bags, gas stove, gas lanterns, and all the other things necessary for camping) ready.

My goal was to go lobstering. Back in those days, you
drove to the Keys one of three ways. You could take US
41 South which goes through the Tamiami Trail or take
Highway 60 East and pick up Highway 27 South. We took
off before the sun came up.

My boat trailer had twin axles with four small trailer tires.
By the time we reached just outside of Brandon, I got a flat
tire. I think it was because the boat was overloaded with gear.
The boat had camping gear, fishing gear, my diving gear, our

luggage, the tent, and everything else in it. There were five of us: Betty, Debbie, Kimberly, Melanie, and me. Oh, there was also our small French poodle.

I got the tire changed, and we were back on the road. By the time I got to the junction of Highway 60 and 27, I had another flat tire. I was extremely fortunate that I still had another spare tire to replace it. By the time I got to Venice, I had the third flat tire. Now, it was late in the morning, and I was able to find an open business to purchase a couple of tires.

We were on our way again. This time, we were cruising along the highway just fine. A huge semi-truck passed us going in the opposite direction. The semi caused a vacuum to tear off my boat top and my side curtains. Normally, I would not have trailered with the boat top and side curtains up, but I did so this time to protect the camping gear and our luggage from the rain, much to my regret.

Upon arrival at Knights Key, I noticed the weather was turning very cloudy, and it was starting to get a little chilly. There was a cold front moving through. Sometimes, Easter break is still chilly, and you experience windy days. We checked into the campground office and got our assigned campsite. All of us chipped in and helped with the tent. The wind was getting increasingly stronger, so I parked the station wagon right behind the tent to help shield it from the wind.

It started to rain, and the wind was so intense that it was driving the rain through the tent wall. I got my picnic canopy and covered the tent with it. That solved the problem, at least for the time being.

It was getting dark. I told the family that we should go to bed fully dressed in the event we must evacuate. The kids were having fun. Betty had a concerned look on her face, and I was concerned also.

To this day, I vividly remember Betty was fixing grilled cheese sandwiches and Campbell's vegetable soup for dinner. After eating, we each got our sleeping bag and air mattress and settled in for the night. I was hoping that tomorrow would bring a sunny day and subsided winds.

At some point during the night, I began to smell poop. You know babies do their business in their diapers, and Melanie was in diapers at the time.

As the wind was howling, I hollered at Betty, "Betty, could you check Melanie's diaper and see if she needs to be changed?"

Her diaper was okay, but she needed to use the potty. After she was through doing her business, Betty handed me the potty, and I decided to just open the tent door and pour it outside. As I poured it, a gust of wind blew the urine in my face.

After that incident, I commented, "I've been rained on and peed on. Now, the only thing left is for me to get crapped on."

I slid back into my sleeping bag, and the odor was now more intense. I grabbed a flashlight and started looking around. I was determined to find where the odor was coming from. I looked around. I happened to shine the light on my jeans and saw that my pant leg was full of dog feces. It seems our poodle was the culprit. At some point, he had crawled into my sleeping bag and done his business. When I went into my sleeping bag earlier, the dog poop had gotten all over my pant leg. You really cannot make this stuff up.

Just before sunrise at 3 or 4 a.m., a Greyhound bus full of spring breakers from Michigan began to set up their tents. As they settled in, it began to pour as if we were in a tropical storm. It was a short but powerful shower. It was so strong that the kids with tents pitched in low areas had their pots, pans, and even sleeping bags floating. Those kids woke up the entire campground trying to gather their belongings.

After that night, we got off to a very slow start the next morning. It was still windy, and the water was cold even with a wetsuit on.

I ended up buying six lobsters to bring home, as we never made it into the water for lobstering. Instead, we decided to head home. This was Easter, and the girls had not experienced their annual Easter egg hunt. Betty, who is very creative, had this brainy idea that we could pull over in a picnic area, and she would boil eggs and dye them with grape Kool-Aid. The girls had fun dying the eggs purple. We then settled in for a long ride home.

I learned an important lesson here. Easter is a time to reflect on the awesome price that our Lord and Savior paid for our salvation. We should have been in church. We would never go camping again on Easter. Easter is to be spent in worship, thanksgiving, and remembrance of the resurrection of our Lord.

Lucky to be Alive

On another occasion diving for lobster, I had put together a trip to Fort Pierce. There were originally four of us going. The weather had been bad. In fact, there was a tropical storm that had just gone up the East Coast of Florida. On the day we were scheduled to leave, two of the fellas bailed out on us. However, my hardcore fishing buddy, Mike Craig, and I decided to go for it. So, we got up early and headed across the state to Fort Pierce.

We checked in at a Holiday Inn, put our luggage in our room, and headed out to the boat ramp. The weather had cleared up somewhat. It was still a little windy, but it was doable. The inlet leading to the ocean from Fort Pierce can be treacherous. To prove my point, let me share with you what happened.

As we headed out the pass, a huge wave swept over the boat and knocked me to the floor. I don't remember if Mike grabbed the steering wheel, but I was able to regroup and grab it myself. By now though, the boat had now turned slightly sideways. This is a dangerous position to be in, as there was another big wave coming.

We finally got through the pass and noticed the visibility of the water was quite good. We headed out to about 60 or 70 feet of water, tossed the anchor, and put on our dive gear. Every diver knows that someone should always stay in the boat. However, we did not want to dive alone, so we went down, secured the anchor, and proceeded to look for fish, lobster, or anything else that might appear. I remember I speared a fish, grabbed a lobster, and turned to find my dive buddy. My dive buddy was nowhere to be found. He was spearfishing and grabbing lobsters too. Soon, I looked at my dive gauge, and I only had 500 pounds of air left in my tank. This is when you should surface and start getting back to the boat. I surfaced, but I didn't see the boat. I looked to my right, and I didn't see the boat. I looked to my left, and I didn't see the boat. At that point, I got a little anxious. One of the waves picked me up, and I spotted the boat. It appeared that the boat was about 50 yards away. The bow of the boat was pointed east, and the stern was facing west. My position was north of that.

I set a course aiming for the front of the boat. As a dive tank gets empty, it becomes very buoyant. I went underwater for a few feet and swam in the direction toward the front of the boat. The waves were coming from the east and pushing me to shore, so I had to compensate for that by not aiming straight for the boat and picking out a spot in front of it. When you dive, you should always put a rope out the back of the boat with some sort of a marker. This is for situations just like this.

I sucked all 500 pounds of air out of the tank. I took my tank off and pushed it in front of me. I was making very little progress. At some point, I took off my weight belt and dropped it. It wasn't long after that I let all my fish and lobster go. Then, I had to let my speargun go. This was life-threatening to me. It was difficult to swim towards the boat with the waves crashing over all the gear, so I had to release every item but my tank and regulator. I remember struggling in the waves crashing over me. I had swallowed some saltwater. I was now using my snorkel. With one last desperate kick of my fins, I was finally able to grab the rope that was out the back of the boat.

During this time, I had not seen Mike Craig and wondered where he was. I tied my tank and regulator off to the end of the rope, and I climbed into the boat. I was getting very seasick. About that time, Mike popped right up by the dive platform at the back of the boat. He asked me how things were going and how I did. He had a clip with some very nice-looking fish and lobster. As he went to toss everything in the boat, a wave picked up the boat. The fish hit the transom and never made it on the boat.

Mike climbed in and asked me where my gear was. I told him I had tied it off to the end of the rope.

He responded, "It's not there. It's drifting away."

Mike proceeded to tie a boat cushion to the anchor rope and released it overboard. He cranked up the engine and went to retrieve my tank, BC, and regulator. Now, we had to go back and get our anchor. As we approached the boat cushion, we saw that the strap on the boat cushion had broken, and the anchor rope was beginning to sink. Mike handed me the steering wheel, walked to the front of the boat, dove in, and retrieved the anchor rope.

I was now seasick. I had a buddy in the water. He had a rope in one hand and was trying to get back to the boat with the wind blowing water in his face and the seas two to three feet. I was attempting to keep the boat from landing on top of him but still trying to keep it close. Mike made it back in the boat with the anchor. We were both exhausted now, so we headed back in. As we came in the pass, there was a picnic area on the right-hand side. I remember beaching the boat, climbing off, lying down on a picnic table, and falling asleep because I was so exhausted. I woke up to a burning sensation. The sun was baking my skin.

It was time to put the boat back on the trailer. I was ready to go home. We pulled up to the Holiday Inn, grabbed our suitcases, and went to check out. We never used the room. I shared our story with the clerk. She was so moved that she did not charge us, and we headed home. Lesson learned: Someone has to stay with the boat.

A Spiritual Happening

After returning home from a trip to the mountains, I experienced something that I have never experienced before. I was exhausted. It was 2 a.m., and I had been towing our camper trailer for 12 hours. I unloaded the truck and rushed to get ready for bed. By that time, I was so wound up that there was no way I could go to sleep. One thing I've learned about my walk with the Lord is that when your body, the temple of the Holy Ghost, is physically exhausted you give the enemy an open door.

"The thief cometh not, but for to steal, and to kill, and to destroy: I am come that they might have life, and that they might have it more abundantly." (John 10:10 KJV).

Jesus tells us that He came that we might have life and have it to the fullest.

I eventually went to bed and had a horrible nightmare. Whether it was a dream or a vision, I cannot tell. Satan was consuming Debbie, our oldest daughter. There was a lovely picture of Debbie on the dresser in our bedroom. Her blonde hair was beautiful, and she was wearing a bright red dress. As I began to shake off what I thought to be a nightmare, I glanced at the picture. There appeared to be a cloud, an oppressive mist or force, surrounding the picture. I knew it wasn't good.

I quickly jumped out of bed and headed towards Debbie's room. As I opened the door, this unnatural oppressive force, this cloud, was blocking my way. With tears in my eyes and a frightened spirit, I remembered what a Sunday school teacher, Jim Aiken, had taught us. The blood of Jesus has the power to repel the enemy. I prayed the blood of Jesus over Debbie, the room, our entire house, and our family. The fog lifted and the Peace of God came all over me. It was a live and real testament to the power. There is power in the blood of Jesus and in His most majestic name.

I knew I had to tell someone, so I called my dad. By now, Chico had grown spiritually. He understood so much more than me.

As I shared my experience, he said, "What you have experienced was a spiritual happening. Learn from it and be cautious not to share this with just anyone. The Lord will direct you when to share and when not to share this experience."

When your body is exhausted and under stress, you open the door for the enemy to rush in to attack you personally or to attack a family member. In my case, it was my daughter, Debbie.

Another Lesson Learned!

About three months after my daughter, Debbie, married Joseph Marchitto, we left for a scheduled vacation to the Florida Keys. We took our camper and a Class C motorhome which belonged to my father-in-law, Capt. Henry Black. Joe towed our boat with the motorhome. We settled in at the Sunshine Key Campground for what we thought was going to be at least a two-week vacation.

I can tell you upfront that this trip was a disaster. We launched the boat at a boat ramp next to the Spanish Harbor Bridge, located just up from Big Pine Key. That day, we made a visit to Looe Key, a beautiful underwater coral reef. Betty, Debbie, Joe, David Sawyer, my other two daughters, and I were on the boat. After a wonderful day of snorkeling and scuba diving, we began the thirty-minute boat ride back to the boat ramp.

We have been avid lobster divers for as long as I can remember. In fact, I had a commercial license to harvest lobster at one point. This meant that I was not limited to the number of lobsters that I could keep. As we neared the Spanish Harbor Bridge, we decided that Joe was going to hang onto the dive platform to look for lobsters. As we neared the bridge, the current was pretty intense. It appeared our boat was headed for a collision with the pylon. I looked back at Joe, made eye contact, and told him I was backing up. He acknowledged that. Between the current and the movement of the boat, Joe's legs went under the platform. I heard a thud and felt on the controls that I had hit something.

I immediately said, "Joe, are you okay?"

He replied, "I think I may have lost a few toes."

It took some discipline to keep from panicking and to try to get everything under control in order to evaluate the injury. I quickly anchored the boat, jumped overboard, and took a look at what had happened. Joe's fin on his right foot had been cut through, as was his dive boot that he had worn under the fin. I took the weights off his weight belt and wrapped the weight belt over his foot. I removed the fin. I climbed back in the boat and muscled Joe over the dive platform and into the boat.

It was getting late. It must have been about 4 p.m. Immediately, I knew what I had to do. I unhitched the trailer from my truck and secured the boat near the boat ramp. Debbie, Joe, and I proceeded to Marathon Community Hospital, also called the Fisherman's Hospital. Betty, David, Kimberly, and Melanie stayed with the boat and all of our equipment.

Upon arrival at the hospital, I rang a doorbell button for assistance.

A voice came over the speaker, "May I help you?"

I told the hospital staff that we had had a boating accident and that the prop from the engine had cut the foot of one of our divers. Keep in mind, Debbie and Joe were newlyweds. Debbie, Joe, and I all heard the individual at the other end of the speaker.

"Possible amputation."

The doctors administered first-aid and some antibiotics but informed us that they did not have the proper facilities or physicians on duty equipped to handle this sort of injury. They were in the process of calling Key West for an ambulance. Key West was approximately 50 miles from where we were in Marathon.

I said, "That is not acceptable."

We agreed on a plan. With the pain medication and the proper bandaging, we could drive Joe to Key West in our Ford F150 truck with a tumbling mat in the back. With this, we would not have to wait for an ambulance to make a round-trip.

We still had the issue of the boat in the water. Before we could head for Key West, we had to secure the boat and get Betty, Kim, Mel, and David back to the campground. I am certain that I must have been driving that truck 80 or 90 miles per hour with my flashers flashing. I was never pulled over by a police officer. If you know the Florida Keys, you know that no one speeds through Big Pine Key without being caught. That night, I didn't get caught.

Upon arrival at the hospital in Key West, I made certain that Debbie and Joe were secure, and Joe was getting the attention he needed. I drove back to the Sunshine Key Campground. In the morning, we planned to relocate our campsite to another campground in Key West. As I was getting ready, I cranked up my truck, and I smelled gas. I popped the hood, and I could see that my fuel pump was spewing gas. That was a definite fire hazard. I took the motorhome, and I believe Betty went with me. This was before the highways and bridges were four lanes. The Seven Mile Bridge was a very narrow two-lane highway. The hubcaps on the motor-home stuck out almost dangerously. I remember moving way over to let a semi-truck come by, causing the hubcaps to rub against the railing on the bridge. It was frightening.

We found an auto parts store in Marathon and purchased the correct fuel pump. This was very early in the morning. We needed to do a lot of work before we could get back to Debbie and Joe. I remember I had to move several components of the engine in order to have enough room to install the fuel pump. We finally found a campground in Key West that would accept pets. We had our poodle with us, so we were turned down at several campgrounds. We settled in with the trailer. We could not take the motorhome because Joe was the driver of the motorhome. We had to arrange for Tom Sawyer, David's dad, to fly into Key West to transport him to the Sunshine Key Campground where the motorhome and boat were located.

I shared with Tom that he would have to drive the motorhome with the boat back to the campground in Key West. We had not seen Debbie or Joe in over 24 hours. We had been in contact with them by phone. The doctors at Key West General Hospital said that Joe would have to have special care, and it had to be done within 48 hours because of the high concentration of bacteria in the saltwater where the accident had occurred. The next morning, we made certain the boat was secure to the motorhome Tom was going to drive back to Tampa. As Tom drove up the incline leading out of the campground, Betty shouted at him to stop. For whatever reason, she decided to check out the trailer hitch. Thank God she did. The welding that held the trailer hitch was rusted out and was all but gone. We had to unhook the boat trailer and find someone in town that could do the welding before the boat could be towed.

Once the welding was complete, Tom was able to get back on the road and head home. As he drove over the Seven Mile Bridge on the return to Tampa, the hubcaps on the motorhome rubbed against the railing on the bridge again. Kimberly was horrified. Later, she said that she thought the motorhome was going to go over the bridge into the water. She had visions of being upside down in the water just as she had recently seen in *The Poseidon Adventure*, a movie about a ship that was struck by a rogue wave and ended up underwater.

Betty and I were left at the campground with the pickup truck and the camper. Upon our arrival at the hospital in Key West, I was informed that we needed to fly Joe to St. Joseph's Hospital in Tampa. There, a surgeon could repair the damage on his foot. We transported Joe to the airport via an ambulance. Betty and I made certain that he and Debbie got on the aircraft. As we waved goodbye, we knew that Joe was going to get the care he so desperately needed.

That afternoon, there were reports of some severe weather headed our way. In fact, it was worse than a tropical storm. Much to our surprise, it had been classified as a hurricane, as we later learned. I immediately purchased a battery-operated radio, taped the windows of our camper, and decided to spend the night and head for home the next day. The winds blew. The lightning and thunder were unbelievable. Visions of the water level rising kept me awake all night. Sunlight peeked through the window. I went outside. The winds had subsided, but I could see numerous boats had sunk during the night. The winds had also torn the awning on our camper. I had to remove the canopy, go into town, and find a shop that repairs canvas boat tops and awnings. I waited while the work was completed.

Meanwhile, Betty was back at the camper securing things for the ride home. Once the canopy was repaired, I headed back to the campground to reinstall it. At that time, Betty informed me that the lawn furniture that we had secured the night before was in 10 feet of water just over the seawall. By now, it was around 4 p.m. I remember heading up the road from Key West and having tire problems on the camper. We turned around and headed towards the Sears auto department in Key West. We had to purchase several tires. Because they did not have them in stock, we had to wait several hours for them to arrive and be installed.

Once again, we were on the road. It had been a long time since we had eaten. I think we missed lunch. We were hungry, so we stopped at a local Kentucky Fried Chicken and got take-out. We went into our camper to eat. All of the lights in the camper went out. Once we got through dinner with flashlights, we headed back up the road. By the time we got past Key Largo, we had to decide as to whether to go home via the Tamiami Trail or Interstate 95 out of Miami.

It rained the entire time. Roads were flooded. I turned on the radio and listened to the weather report that was advising motorists to not use US 41, the Tamiami Trail, due to some of the road being underwater as much as three feet. By that time, it was late, eight or nine at night. We drove up US 1, picked up US 95 North, and then headed west towards Tampa on a very dark and lonely road. We went through Yeehaw Junction, Mulberry, Brandon, and finally Tampa. We arrived home around 3 a.m. That was an awfully long day.

Meanwhile, Debbie and Joe had checked into St. Joseph's Hospital. They had stabilized Joe and were preparing to attempt to save his toes and a small portion of his foot that had been injured. The game plan was to graft his right foot onto his left calf. This would assure blood flow. Medical bills were piling up. His doctor's bedside manner left much to be desired. I entered the elevator on the way home after visiting Joe, and Joe's doctor was riding the same elevator. I confronted him with the insensitivity that he was showing to this newlywed couple, as the couple had been traumatized and were concerned about finances.

Joe had just started working with General Telephone Company, so insurance was an issue. I don't remember the doctor's name, but I do remember that after our chance meeting on the elevator he reduced his bill drastically. This was another example of how God took care of us from the beginning of this ordeal to the very special way it all ended. The doctor salvaged Joe's foot and toes, even though Joe now grows hair on the bottom of his foot because of the skin graft. I learned another hard lesson through this experience. Stay away from towing people while passing under a bridge. When I'm driving my boat to this day, I have visions of Joe's foot being almost severed every time I bump the bottom in shallow water or hit an obstacle in the water.

Bimini

While principal of Bayshore Christian School, we became friends with the Robinson family–Ken, Chris, Julie, and Kenny. Ken was the owner of Robinson Electric, a Christian company. The gospel of Jesus Christ was openly shared in their workplace. It was not uncommon for people to pray for one another. Ken was an avid fisherman and boater. His daughter, Julie, and my daughter, Melanie, were good friends. Our families developed a close relationship.

Mr. Robinson and I began talking about taking our two boats across the Gulf Stream to Bimini. He had a 28 foot Sea Ray, and I had a 20 foot Wellcraft that carried only 40 gallons of fuel. Before planning got too far ahead, I decided to share what we were doing with Betty.

I came home one day and said, "Betty, we're going to Bimini."

Her response was, "What airlines are we taking?"

I said, "We're not flying. We're going by boat."

She wanted to know where Bimini was located. It is literally a dot on the map.

Betty responded, "What happens if we miss the island?"

I answered, "The next coast is Africa, and we certainly don't have enough fuel to get there."

That is not what Betty wanted to hear.

All plans were made, and it was now time to trailer our boats across the state to a marina on the East Coast of Florida for our departure. We rented a hotel room, spent the night, and got up early the next morning to begin our journey.

The crossing was relatively smooth. Within a short period of time, the island was in sight. The crossing is close to 50 miles. Once you get to Bimini, you have to check into immigration and state what your businesses is in Bimini. Our oldest daughter, Debbie, had researched the place that I had reserved for our stay. It did not meet her expectations. Without us knowing, she rented a big house on a hill. It was on the beach and came with a maid and a swimming pool.

I only had capacity for 40 gallons of fuel, 20 gallons on each side of the boat. Upon arrival at Bimini and after checking into immigration, we proceeded to gas up, only to find that there was no fuel on the island. There had been a major fishing tournament the week before, and all available fuel had been consumed. They were waiting for the Shell Oil barge to deliver fuel. For the first few days, we were land-locked and limited to snorkeling just off the beach.

Debbie, Kim, Melanie, and Matthew flew over on Chalk Airlines in a seaplane. Later, Debbie told us the windows leaked and water came into the plane as they landed.

The remaining days in Bimini were filled with great fishing and snorkeling. The water in Bimini is crystal clear and has abundant fish life and beautiful coral reefs.

On our way home, the seas were rolling seas. You had to throttle forward to go up the hill of water and then throttle back to keep from burying the nose of your boat into the water. Shortly after we took off from Bimini, a large Coast Guard cutter came between our two boats. With a large megaphone, they ordered us to turn off our engines, as we were to be boarded.

The Coast Guard put out two rubber rafts, each containing three Coast Guardsmen. I took out my Nikon camera and began taking pictures of them coming towards me.

Mrs. Betty was a nervous wreck. One of the young Coast Guardsmen was a little on the heavy side. As he tried to board my 20-foot boat, he almost fell in. He asked a series of questions while filling out a questionnaire.

The seas were rolling. Some of those rollers were eight to nine feet tall. I can be prone to seasickness even though I take medication for it. Having to sit and answer questions from the young Coast Guardsman, I remember not feeling well.

I said to him, "I hope you're almost done. I think I'm about to barf all over you."

He immediately replied, "Mr. Valdes, we're done. Have a good trip."

Mr. Robinson was not so lucky. The Coast Guard was looking for drugs and illegal paraphernalia. Mr. Robinson's Sea Ray had a closed-in cabin and bunks. The Coast Guard went through every cabinet, tossing things around and looking under everything that they could possibly look under. After not finding any drugs, they finished and gave him a citation for not having his life preservers readily accessible. Normally, you would only get a citation for not having life preservers or not having the correct number of life preservers.

Abaco Islands

The following year, the Robinson family and the Valdes family planned to go to the Abaco Islands. We had bought a bigger boat. Debbie, Joe, and I partnered on buying a big enough boat with high sides to accommodate our new grandson. We bought a 24-foot Mako with high railings, a small cabin, and a small shower. We took the boat on a trial run prior to buying it. Matthew's dad, Joe, and I went out with half or little less than half a tank of gas. The boat appeared to run fine. It had a 225-horse powered Yamaha.

The boat was a sled the first time we took a group fishing. We had four guys, our gear and dive tanks, and several large coolers filled with ice, food, and drinks. It was terribly slow, exceedingly difficult to get up on a plane. We immediately began to look for a larger engine and purchased a counter-rotating 275 HP Yamaha.

I had approximately one week to break in the engine. On the fourth day, two pistons shot right out through the engine cover. Yes, the engine was covered under warranty, but it would not be ready in time for us to take the boat to the Abaco Islands. By this time, Mr. Robinson had a larger boat, and he felt that we could all fit in his boat, as some of our party were flying over.

We spent the night at the same marina from our Bimini trip. That evening, the air conditioner on the boat was blowing very cold air. Betty was looking for a blanket, but she could not find one. Betty has always been able to adapt, adjust, and overcome. She took the pillowcase off the pillow and crawled into the pillowcase. In the morning, she mentioned to Ken how cold it was and how it was not possible to find a blanket in the dark. He reached over the bunk and opened the cabinet where all the blankets were stored. The blankets had been right above her the entire time.

The rest of the family flew into Marsh Harbor. We rented a house on Little Abaco. On the crossing over to the main island, we stopped to check in with immigration and to refuel. The crossing over is 50 miles. Then, it's island hopping for approximately 100 miles to Little Abaco.

We arrived at immigration and were ready to check-in. We were told that the person in charge had left for lunch. Approximately two hours later, he showed up. Keep in mind, we could not fuel the boat until after we had checked in with immigration. These are steps that must be taken in that order. After we checked in, we headed to the gas pump, only to learn that that person had just gone to lunch. So, we wasted approximately three hours and were now looking at spending the night on the boat.

Betty always does her homework. She made sure we had all the necessary books and charts needed for the trip. There were certain markers we were to watch for in order to get us to the house we had rented. One of the books showed a photograph of three young native boys sitting on the end of a dock. We were told that there was a restaurant nearby that dock. The restaurant consisted of a house on stilts and a dock. When we arrived, there were three native boys sitting on the dock. To this day, Betty swears that those were the same boys in the photograph in the booklet we had been consulting.

I had my mind set on having lobster for dinner that evening. We found out that there was only one entrée on the menu. It was fried chicken and was served with black-eyed peas and rice. Everyone ordered, and it was very, very tasty.

I asked, "What's for dessert?"

The lady, the proprietor, said, "I have some coconut pie."

She did not say coconut cream pie. This is what I had envisioned. She brought out the pie covered with aluminum foil because we planned to eat it later. When we got back in the boat and were ready to sample the pie, I was shocked. It was a grainy type of pie that looked somewhat like pecan pie. It had brown specks that resembled pepper on top. The lady had grated the coconut with the brown skin on it and used that to make the pie. I am not sure of the other ingredients; however, it was incredibly good even though it did not look very appetizing.

The house we rented was up on a hill. It belonged to an ambassador. There were 15 of us making this trip: the Robinson family, the Valdes family, the Joe Marchitto family, and Danette Miranda, Kim's friend. This was a large house, big enough to accommodate everyone. However, we were not aware that it came equipped with bees. The girls began checking out the rooms to see which ones they would occupy, and they noticed some bees flying around in one of the rooms.

We did not have bug spray to kill the bees, so the girls sprayed them with hairspray. The bees came crashing down.

We kept hearing a loud humming sound. Upon further investigation, we went outside only to find the largest beehive that I have ever seen. It was attached to a corner near the roof of the house. The hive was approximately three feet long and two feet wide. Needless to say, the bedroom with the bees was not used.

We adjusted and were ready for the week. One day, Kenny took Matthew, Melanie, and Julie on his dad's rubber dinghy for a boat ride. Not long after, all of us could see that the weather was changing rapidly, and dark skies appeared. Debbie became concerned about Matthew, as she thought that they should have been back already. She proceeded to take a 15-foot Boston Whaler that was tied to a dock. She had no idea who it belonged to.

She cranked up the motor and began searching for those who had left in the dinghy. We later teased her about "stealing" a boat. To this day, Debbie will tell you that she "borrowed" it. All were safe, and the weather passed on by. That was a good trip, a great experience, and a real adventure.

Close Encounter

One time in November, Ken Robinson called.

He asked, "Herman, would you like to go fishing?"

With me, "fishing" is the magic word. Ken informed me that the weather had broken. There was a window in the weather that might allow us to go offshore fishing from Anna Maria Island in his Sea Ray boat.

From the beginning, the boat's engine did not sound right. There were some noises that were not common on Ken's boat. We were approximately 15 to 20 miles due west off Anna Maria Island. The weather started turning bad again. It appeared that there was a cold front moving in. It got cloudy and began raining lightly. It was beginning to get chilly.

As we started to make our way back, we got as far as Southwest Pass, the pass between Egmont Key and Anna

Maria Island. The engine just quit. To no avail, we did all of the things we knew to troubleshoot the problem. Ken got on the marine radio and summoned Sea Tow. Meanwhile, we needed to anchor the boat, secure it, and settle in for the increasing winds and rain.

It was now beginning to get dark. The towing company would take approximately two hours to get to us. They start their clock from when they leave the dock to the time they return with you. It seemed like an eternity before the tow boat reached us. We had to climb through a hatch, pull in the anchor rope, and secure the tow rope. The tow rope was quite long.

I performed that task and got soaking wet. There were four or five grown men inside the boat cabin, being towed by a much smaller boat going awfully slow. We were headed north and settled in for the long ride home.

It was necessary to cross the Egmont channel in order to get to Maximo Marina. The moon was not visible. It was pitch dark. When towing another vessel, one shortens the rope in order to make the turns. We did not know there was a large tanker ship going west in our path as we approached the Egmont channel going north.

We were on a collision course. This small boat was towing a larger boat with a long rope between the two. The tow boat made a right-hand 90° angle turn with the boat being towed and continuing to go straight.

At some point, the rope straightened, and we could now see some lights. We were in the cabin and not aware of this huge ship that was in our path. I remember telling the guys that I could see the Sunshine Skyway Bridge lights. I went to the front hatch to take a look. The lights I saw were not the Sunshine Skyway Bridge lights but the lights on a ship that appeared to only be about 10 yards from us. It seemed that close at least.

I remember saying to everyone, "Grab your life preserver." Everyone kept asking, "Why do we have to grab one?"

Due to the urgent sound of my voice, they began to get very curious. When they looked out of the cabin, they saw this massive ship that was so close it seemed we could reach out and touch it. That was a close call. I thought for sure that I was going to die that night. I had visions of getting chewed up by a massive propeller in frigid waters.

As we approached Maximo Marina, the tow boat shortened its rope in order to navigate the channel and the entrance to the marina.

We had taken off from the boat ramp near the Gandy Bridge in Tampa Bay and ended up at a marina in St. Petersburg. I believe Ken's wife drove her car to Maximo Marina in St. Petersburg and gave us a ride home. The next day, Ken had to deal with taking care of the boat and finding out what the mechanical problems were.

Another Close Encounter

On another occasion, we were diving for stone crab claws just south of the main draw of the Sunshine Skyway Bridge. At some point, I became separated from my diving partner. You must dive this bridge during the slack tide. As the tide changes, the current is so powerful that it becomes very difficult to swim from piling to piling.

I had caught my share of stone crabs and had removed their claws. All of a sudden, I heard the sound of a ship's propeller. The sound had started off faint, but it slowly got louder. It was steadily getting closer. At that point, no one could have convinced me that I was in an area that was safe and away from the ship. In my mind, I had worked my way to the middle of the bridge, the area where the ships and boats cross. I was convinced a ship was coming.

I did not dare surface for fear that the ship would be right there. I remember grabbing a rock and being in a fetal position with fear totally encompassing me. I just knew I was going to die. You know that cliché about "sweating bullets." I was literally sweating in my mask. I know for sure I was even sweating in the water.

This diving experience took place not too long after the Sunshine Skyway Bridge disaster. A ship ran into the bridge, and people lost their lives in the water. There were massive amounts of twisted steel on the bottom of the bay. Swimming through the wreckage looking for stone crabs was eerie. The sound of the propeller began to get fainter and fainter. As I slowly ascended, my head cleared the surface. To my surprise, I was nowhere near the center of the bridge. There are no words that can describe the fear I experienced at the moment. I felt I was in the path of the ship.

Weathering the Storm

David Small, a close friend of mine, had a 24-foot tri-hull Wellcraft named *Serendipity*. David, Tom Mosca, and I went fishing for kingfish. Kingfish migrate north and south. Twice a year, we have a run of kingfish off our Gulf beaches. We started our trip around 4 a.m. We met at a local marina near Tarpon Springs, launched the boat and proceeded to gas up.

The boat had several rod holders built into the gunwales. When David took the gas cap off, he did not pay very close attention and placed the nozzle of the gas hose in the rod holder instead. He proceeded to set the mechanism on the gas hose to automatically shut off when the tank was full.

The marina was almost empty. There were not many people in the diner, so a quick breakfast sounded good. The *Serendipity* was an inboard/outboard. The engine was on the inside of the boat, and the outdrive was on the outside on the transom. When we got back to the boat after breakfast, the fumes of gas were strong, and we realized what had happened.

I proceeded to lift the engine cover off, only to see gasoline as high as the cables that were hooked to the battery. Had we not looked when we did and hit the ignition, we would have all been toast, burnt toast. We might not have survived.

One of the attendants took the boat out of the water with a giant forklift and put it on davits, so we could take care of the issue with the gasoline.

As the forklift lifted the boat, approximately 60 gallons of fuel that was in the bilge rushed to the front. The boat almost tipped off the forklift. David had a side job selling cleaning products, and he happened to have quite a bit of the products in his vehicle. We used the product to clean the boat; however, the fuel had to be drained from the boat before any cleaning could be done.

By now, it was almost 10 a.m. We started our day at 4 a.m. When grouper fishing, you typically try to catch the early morning bite or the afternoon bite. We headed out anyway. God is so good! David, Tom, and I caught more than our share of fish that day. Praise be to God! He took care of us with the fuel issue as well.

On that same day, there were storms everywhere as were coming in. Right in front of us, there was a dark, dark curtain of rain that caused an almost total absence of sunlight. In fact, I remember the other boats had gone into the same storm, and we could no longer see them. My fear was that we would run into one of them. I remember telling Tom Mosca to grab his life preserver. Tom had had a few beers that day and had fallen asleep in the cabin. When I woke him to tell him to get his life preserver, he asked what was going on. I gave him a quick summary.

He said, "Just give me another beer. If we're going down, I don't want to know it."

Family Stories

W HEN BETTY WAS PREGNANT WITH our first
daughter, Debbie, we lived in a small apartment
that was attached to Betty's mom and dad's house. It had a
small living room and bedroom in one room. It also had a
small eat-in kitchen and a bathroom. We had a brand new
Chevrolet Corvair Monza. To this day, I don't know how we
afforded it. The engine was in the back. One was supposed
to be able to drive the car on the beach through sand and
obstacles because of the torque and front-wheel drive.

In Port Tampa, Betty's dad captained a 98-foot steam-op-
erated tugboat. We boarded the tugboat many times on dates
to the Sunshine Skyway Bridge to bring ships into the port.
In the same area the tugboat was docked, there were three
islands that had been joined by pumping beach sand and
mud between them. We had been to this area many times,
enough that I now wanted to try driving the Corvair on

the beach to see if it would do everything the commercials said it would.

My brother-in-law, Clifford Sawyer, whom everyone called "Tom Sawyer," and I took off in the new car. We were driving on the beach and doing quite well. Suddenly, the car just sank into the mud. I mean it sank. The wheels were half buried. The floorboards were even with the mud. This beautiful new car was about to be ruined. The tide was coming in, and the mud was really soft. Because of where the car was located in the mud, a carjack could not be used.

A ship was docked nearby, and several of its sailors were walking on the beach. They noticed that we were in trouble. Several of the men went into the trees on the island and found several pine trees that had been cut into logs. We used the lever system to dislodge the car from the mud. We put a log in front of the car, placed the other log under the car and over the big log, and pried down, thereby lifting the front end of the car. Some of the other guys pushed it on solid ground. Then, we did the same at the rear end of the car.

At this point, the tide was lapping at the car door. We managed to get the car out just in time and drove home. When Betty heard what had happened, I thought she was going to have the baby right then. We had to pull the wheels off the car and hose down the brakes and the rotors, as salt water can be hazardous to an automobile. What a fiasco that was! We decided not to take any other chances. After some time, we traded in the car.

Engine Down

Another time, I went out with Jim Morris, Betty's cousin, on a flat-bottomed wooden boat with a 25-horse outboard motor made by Montgomery Ward. The brand name of the engine was Wizard. We were going along quite well. All of a sudden, the whole engine came off the transom. Somehow, I managed to hang on to it. I did not let go of the throttle. It was a tiller engine, so you steered with a tiller and not a steering wheel. The engine was on its side and continued to run.

I think my right arm must have been stretched to its maximum. Jim could do nothing but laugh. He laughed so hard I thought he was going to pee in his pants. The engine was saved. Betty's dad, who owned the boat, never found out about it.

The Joys of Being a Grandparent

After raising three daughters and coaching everyone else's sons, I just knew that somewhere down the line we would have some boys in the family. We have a total of five beautiful grandchildren – three boys and two girls. Here are my grandchildren in chronological order. Matthew, Amanda, Michael, Jordan, and Allison. Our three great-grandchildren are all boys – Keegan, Truett, and Rowan.

When Matthew calls and invites me to go offshore fishing, we go anywhere from 30 to 70 miles offshore. I drop everything to be with my grandsons.

On a particular trip around 4 p.m., Matthew, Jordan, Cameron (Jordan's friend), and I met at the marina. We loaded all our equipment on the boat and headed to the house of Matthew's friend, who has a large ice machine and allows Matthew to use it.

We loaded the fish boxes with ice and placed our food and drinks in another ice chest. We settled in, as we were going to spend the night. The boat ride takes approximately two hours. I carry a beanbag chair, as it makes the boat ride much more comfortable. This particular evening was cold, very cold. We fished and caught our limit of Mango Snapper and Yellowtail Snapper. The bite was on. Around midnight or 1 a.m., we decided to call it quits and get a few hours of shut eye. I was watching Matthew and Jordan, thinking of how truly blessed I am.

In the morning, we continued to look for grouper. Almost immediately, we hooked and landed seven groupers in the range of about 15 pounds each. They were out of season though and had to be released. We caught numerous American Red Snappers and three extremely healthy sharks. Each shark was approximately 200 pounds. There was a Bull Shark, a Black Tip Shark, and a Tiger Shark. Each put up a pretty aggressive battle.

After hooking and landing the sharks, we caught a lot of Amberjacks in the 40-50 pound class. However, these were out of season too, and had to be released. We caught a Cobia that weighed approximately 60 pounds. Matthew had to shoot and kill it before bringing it on the boat. After they're caught, Cobia can appear to be exhausted but then get a second wind. They will tear up your boat.

The fishing trip was very productive. The boat ride in was pleasant. The evening was serene. The time spent with my two grandsons was invaluable.

While I was enjoying being with two of my grandsons, my third grandson, Michael, was finishing his senior year at Florida State University. Michael is pursuing a law degree at Cornell University in upstate New York. It is a prestigious opportunity for Michael. We are so immensely proud of him.

Camping

On the way in from this fishing trip, I was reflecting on a camping trip that our family had taken to Rainbow River. This was also during cold weather. Amanda, Allison, and Melanie went with us and stayed with Betty in the camper, as it had an exceptionally good heating system and nice accommodations. The two boys, Michael and Jordan, and I slept in a tent set up outside of the camper.

Herman and grandsons Michael and Jordan camping at Rainbow River.

I challenged the boys to make a fire by rubbing sticks together. I also challenged them to be clean and neat and to keep everything in order in the tent. I would come by and hold inspections just like in the military. Michael and Jordan stood at attention at each side of the entrance to the tent. I would inspect the tent. If the tent did not meet my expectations, each boy would do 20 push-ups. I had a great time. I'm not sure whether the boys did, but they still talk about it to this day. Special times with your grandchildren are a gift from God.

Anniversary Trip

July of 2018 was the best! My bride and I rented a house in Marathon to celebrate our 58th wedding anniversary with our family.

At the time, I was a 78-year-old avid fisherman. I was overjoyed to have the opportunity to do some fishing in Marathon with Matthew, Michael, and Jordan. We fished from Matthew's 28-foot Contender. The seas were calm. The winds were three to five knots. We set our course towards the Marathon Hump, as Matt wanted to do some deep drops and catch a Tile Fish, a Queen Snapper, or maybe even a Snowy Grouper. That did not happen, but we did get into some Blackfin Tuna while doing vertical jigging. Then, Mahi Mahi started to show up.

We began this adventure late in the afternoon. It was now 6:30 p.m. When the Mahi made an appearance, it was game on. It looked like a fire drill. The four of us hooked up on fish at the same time. These were nice fish in the 10-to-12-pound range. Then, some larger fish showed up. We began to chum to keep them around the boat.

I was fishing with my old 3500 Shimano Bait Runner with a 20-pound test fishing line. I was free-lining chunks of Bonito and Ballyhoo when this monster Mahi grabbed my bait. For the next 30 minutes or so, we fought and chased down the fish. Matt is an experienced captain and is always well prepared. He had his new 10-foot gaff. Soon, we had this beauty on board. It weighed almost 51 pounds.

Meanwhile, Jordan hooked up and landed a 42 pounder. Michael was hooked up with a very unusual blue Mahi. I'm told that these are very rare. Everyone caught lots of fish. Besides Mahi, we caught numerous tuna in the four- to six-pound class. These are called footballs due to their shape.

We started home about 8:30 p.m. Soon, it was dark. As I reclined in my bean bag chair, I looked up at the sky. I thought about how blessed I was to have my wife of 58 years, a wonderful family, and the experience of this awesome fishing trip with my grandsons. It doesn't get any better than this.

Grandson Matthew with 51 lb. Mahi

Grandson Jordan with 42 lb. Mahi

Grandson Michael with unusual blue Mahi

Time with My Girls

I make certain I spend some special time with my two granddaughters. I schedule a date with Amanda and Allison during the Christmas season. I take the girls to get their nails done. Then, we go to lunch. After that, it's shopping for Grandma's Christmas gifts. I look forward to this every year.

Blessings

God is an awesome God. God is good all the time. All the time, God is good. God does not make junk. He created us in His own image. When we accept Christ, we become part of the body of Christ. Jesus sits at the right hand of the Father. We are joint heirs with Him. We are royalty. We are the King's kids. Just like the royalty in England, King's kids are educated in the absolute best schools. They have military training and are highly disciplined, and they are held to a higher standard. That's what we are. We are King's kids.

I am so blessed that God has allowed me to have such a wonderful family and has allowed me to see my great-grandchildren. None of this would have been possible without the most precious lady in my life, my bride of 60 years at the time of this writing. I am so thankful and grateful that God healed Betty from breast cancer and allowed her to enjoy our family.

Matthew is a graduate of St. Petersburg College with a Bachelor's in Business Administration. He is the service manager for Central Marine and is married to a very precious woman, Destiny. Amanda is a graduate of Florida State University with a Master's in Early Childhood Education. She is teaching at the University of South Florida and is working on her doctorate. Michael graduated from Florida State University and is in his third year of law school at Cornell University. Jordan is a graduate of the University of South Florida with a Bachelor's in Business Administration. Allison currently attends the University of South Florida.

There are so many things I felt I needed to include in this book but did not. For example, I don't spend much time speaking of my precious wife, who taught school for 28 years, and my three wonderful and successful daughters. These four ladies are the joy of my life. Deborah McGinty, Kimberly Mirabella, and Melanie Humenansky are special ladies. I'm so proud of them. They were involved in my coaching career as statisticians, ball girls, and hostesses. My wife and three girls have accumulated over 10,000 hours of gym time.

Daughters L-R, Melanie, Kim and Debbie with Betty.

Debbie is a University of South Florida graduate and is a highly successful real estate agent. Kim is a University of Tampa graduate and serves as the Director of Sales for Southeast Government Markets with Verizon Wireless. Melanie Humenansky graduated from the University of South Florida. She pursued a coaching and administrative career in education. Melanie's teams have won four State Championships in volleyball. She was selected to take over as Head of School at Bayshore Christian School after I retired. My three daughters and their husbands have always been there for me. They were there for their wonderful mother, a cancer survivor, during difficult times with support, encouragement, and prayer.

christ as savior

I N OCTOBER OF 1975 AT the age of 35, I was challenged with the scripture in Revelation 3:15-16 from the King James version of the Bible.

"I know thy works, that thou art neither cold nor hot: I would thou wert cold or hot. So then because thou art luke-warm, and neither cold nor hot, I will spue thee out of my mouth." (Rev.3:15-16 KJV)

The word "spue" in Greek and Latin, literally means to vomit. In other words, someone being lukewarm makes God sick. That was me. I wasn't turned off and I wasn't turned on. I was straddling the fence, one foot on cold and one foot on hot. It was clear that I needed to ask Jesus to forgive me of my sins, come into my heart and make me a turned-on Christian. You too, can get off the fence-straddling position by accepting Christ as your savior.

We go through life and receive many titles. For me some of the titles were teacher, coach, principal, Reverend, etc. In the year 2008, I was ordained by the Agape Evangelistic Mission Inc. I was sponsored by one of my mentors, Dallas Albritton. Of all the titles I've received, the title of Reverend was the most meaningful. It has opened many doors for me to do God's work.

Herman and mentor, Dallas Albritton at ordination ceremony.

I have listed three scriptures that I found helpful in leading me to Christ. Since 1975, this event in my life has been responsible for hundreds having their names written in the Lamb's Book of Life. The scriptures are as follows: John 14:6, Acts 16:30-31, and John 3:16.

In John 14:6, Jesus tells Thomas the way to the Father...

"Jesus answered, "I am the way and the truth and the life. No one comes to the Father except through me." (John 14:6 NIV)

In other words, no one gets to the father, except through accepting Jesus as their savior.

When the jailer asked of Paul and Silas, "Sirs, what must I do to be saved?" in Acts 16:30-31, the response was...

"Believe on the Lord Jesus, and you will be saved- you and your household." (Acts 16:30-31 NIV)

In John 3:16, it states...

"For God so loved the world that he gave his one and only Son, that whoever believes in him shall not perish but have eternal life." (John 3:16 NIV)

I would be remiss if I did not invite you to accept Christ as your Lord and Savior with the promise of eternal life. It's as easy as three simple steps.

Acknowledge that you are a sinner and ask for forgiveness.

Repent of your sins.

Ask Jesus to come into your heart and make you the person He would have you to be.

It is my prayer that you would become a child of God by asking Jesus into your heart. May Jesus Christ bless you richly as you invite Him into your life.

Blessings,
Coach Herman Valdes

Almost 40 years ago, I believe God spoke to my heart that I was to write a book. Shortly thereafter, He gave me the title, **Chico and the Coach.** One of my friends and former pastor, Bruce Williams, encouraged me and suggested I try the "Dragon Naturally Speaking" software which is a voice-to-text program. That's how I got started. This book was "God-driven" and "Holy-Spirit-led."

There is so much more I would like to have written about, specifically my time spent at Bayshore Christian School where I was Head of School and basketball coach for a total of 15 years. As my wife tells me, "You cannot include everything, or it would take 80 years."

That is another book perhaps.

CPSIA information can be obtained
at www.ICGtesting.com
Printed in the USA
JSHW010731140421
13507JS00004B/67